SOUTHERN FRIED CRIME

Ron Franscell
Stephanie Cook
Gregg Olsen
Rebecca Morris

Copyright 2015 by
Ron Franscell, Stephanie Cook, Gregg Olsen, and Rebecca Morris,
All Rights Reserved
Book Cover Design by BEAUTeBOOK
No part of this publication may be reproduced, stored in a retrieval system, or transmitted, in any form or by any means, electronic, mechanical, photocopying, recording, or otherwise, without the written permission of the authors.
Published by Notorious USA

TABLE OF CONTENTS

NIGHTMARE AT NOON 1

- From the Notorious USA Team 7
- The Lost Boys 9
- Do you know this boy? 25
- The Darkest Tower.. 27
- Nightmare at Noon 53
- Tanya Reid.. 81

EVIL AT THE FRONT DOOR 101

- From the Notorious USA Team 103
- EXECUTED FOR LOVE 107
  - *Photo Archive I*... *118*
- DEATH FROM ABOVE 121
  - *Photo Archive II*.. *152*
- EVIL ON THE FRONT DOOR.. 154
  - *Photo Archive III*... *181*
- A FLOOD OF EVIDENCE.. 183
  - *Photo Archive IV*... *192*

BLACK WIDOW IN A PURE WHITE DRESS................................... 195

- Introduction 197
- Black Widow in a Pure White Dress... 199
- The Good Daughter 208
- The Murderous Middle School Teacher 227
- The Last Breath.. 242
- Photo Archive.. 253
- About the Authors.. 259

NIGHTMARE AT NOON

Ron Franscell
and
Gregg Olsen

Copyright 2015 by Gregg Olsen and Ron Franscell
All Rights Reserved
Book Cover Design by BEAUTeBOOK
Map by Brad Arnesen
No part of this publication may be reproduced, stored in a retrieval system, or transmitted, in any form or by any means, electronic, mechanical, photocopying, recording, or otherwise, without the written permission of the authors.
Published by Notorious USA

From the Notorious USA Team

WELCOME TO THE LATEST INSTALLMENT in the *New York Times* bestselling series of stories about America's most notorious criminals.

That's right. No matter where you live, you're in the middle of Notorious USA.

Everything is bigger in Texas—especially crime. We're teaming up to tell the stories of a serial killer who slaughtered more people than any other psychopath of his day... without ever being noticed; two of America's most shocking mass murders and how their grim echoes still linger today; and the chilling tale of a mother so desperate for attention that she murdered one of her children and repeatedly tried to suffocate the other.

Don't miss *Bodies of Evidence, Darkest Waters, Overkill* and other box sets available as an eBook on most formats, as well as in paperback and as an audio book.

Your crime scribes,

Ron Franscell
Gregg Olsen

The Lost Boys

Serial killer Dean Corll and the Houston Mass Murders

Dean Corll at home

The morgue cooler was so full she couldn't walk in. Standing just inside the heavy door, the cold stink of it washed over Dr. Sharon Derrick, the Harris County Medical Examiner's new forensic pathologist. She was hired to work with organ tissues, but she'd been permitted to work some cold cases in her spare time. She hadn't been with the ME's office very long when she donned her scrubs, left her safe, little office, and went down to the first-floor cooler, where a security guard helped her horse open the heavy door.

It was an alien place to her. Not just the unpleasant, oiled death spunk that spilled out of the body bags and plastic tubs stacked everywhere. Not just the drizzle of condensation—droplets certainly containing invisible particles of human flesh—that fell from the whitewashed ceiling into her hair. Not even the piercing cold that couldn't stop but only slowed the rot inside. She could smell it.

It was the idea that she was suddenly surrounded by questions in search of answers.

The cooler was full of corpses, some fleshed, some just bones. Organized but deathly. Over here, open metal trays were stacked five-tall, each cradling a white body bag. There, gurney tables with more body bags. On one side, shelves were crammed with stained boxes, scrawled with names and numbers.

Just below eye-level on one shelf, she spied a label, HOUSTON MASS MURDERS, with only a case number.

She knew about that case. She had long family ties to the Heights neighborhood, the epicenter of Houston's worst and most perverse serial killing. She was about the enter high school when the whole sordid crime story spilled out. Nearly thirty teenage boys tortured, raped and killed by a sadistic freak between 1970 and 1973, and buried by his teenage henchmen in a rented boat-storage unit, on a remote beach, and in the dark woods of Southeast Texas. Cops dug them all up. She didn't know, though, that questions still lingered in 2006—more than thirty years later.

Derrick gingerly opened the lids of four boxes. They all contained dirty bones, bits of clothing, ropes, and other grisly grave matter.

And none had a name or a face.

Four boys who might have come from her

neighborhood. Who might have been a lot like the boys she'd dated in high school. Who were somebody's sons or brothers. She felt a strange kinship with them.

And now Sharon Derrick ached to know who they were.

Dean Corll had a way with kids. Particularly teenage boys. And especially the ones who felt they didn't belong, or who were misunderstood at home, or got into occasional trouble.

Neighbors knew him as a soft-spoken, thirtysomething bachelor who was friendly, well-groomed, and fastidious. He had a girlfriend whose kids called him "Daddy." He worked as an electrician, although after a short stint in the Army, he managed his mom's candy store in the Heights, a dowdy, old Houston neighborhood that by the 1970s had seen better days.

The Corll Candy Company sat across the street from an elementary school, and Dean loved to hand out bits of candy to the kids. Soon, he put a pool table in back for the older boys, to whom he gave rides on his motorcycle. He rigged a stereo to blast rock music from his trailer next door. And he outfitted a white van with couches, carpeting and surfboard racks so he could take some of those teenagers on weekend beach outings.

Those boys loved Dean. He knew the turmoil inside. He knew the white-boy jive in the backwater neighborhoods where they lived. He spoke their language. He was a fun guy. He was The Candy Man.

But there was nothing sweet about Dean Corll—a pedophile and sadistic killer who might have been luring teenage boys to their deaths for years.

By 1970, the aging Corll employed two young "helpers" to trap his victims, paying them to find victims to satisfy Corll's bloodlust.

His accomplices—teenage dropouts Wayne Henley and David Brooks—were paid at least $200 for each young boy they lured to his various houses. In one, a modest, unremarkable suburban bungalow, he'd built a torture chamber, outfitted with a plank to which victims could be handcuffed, a large knife, ropes, bizarre sex toys, guns, and sheets of plastic over the carpeted floor to deflect splattering blood. The room also contained a large wooden crate with airholes.

Here, Corll's victims suffered unspeakably: objects were inserted into their rectums, glass rods slid into their penises, and all were sodomized, beaten, and terrorized.

Corll's system was frighteningly efficient.

Many of the boys were picked at random off the streets; some were friends of Henley or Brooks, who had a cool, easy way with other boys. At least two sets of brothers were killed by Corll and his henchmen. In fact, many of his victims had connections to others, but nobody ever suspected their ghastly links. Most lived in the Heights or an adjoining neighborhood. And nobody had ever noticed how the teenage boys of the Heights seemed to be disappearing with unusual frequency.

When Corll's sado-sexual urges were satisfied, the boys were strangled or shot, then their corpses were buried in secret mass graves—all only about two feet deep—on the beach at nearby High Island, near a cabin on Lake Sam Rayburn, or in Corll's rented boat shed in southwest Houston.

It all crashed to a halt on August 3, 1973, when Henley brought two friends, including a girl, to Corll's house and an argument erupted. When it was over, Henley had shot Corll six times. The serial killer was dead.

But one of America's most surreal crimes was about to

be revealed to a shocked nation.

Corll's victims were found in three different mass graves: four in St. Augustine on Lake Sam Rayburn in East Texas; seven on the beach at High Island and 17 buried in Stall 11 at the Houston boathouse.

Within days, investigators had unearthed 27 corpses before abruptly ending their digs. In 1983, a 28th decomposed body was found—overlooked in 1973—but even today almost nobody believes Corll's true death toll will ever be known.

For one, co-workers at the sweet shop remember him digging odd holes where he claimed to be burying bad batches of candy. Might they have been other graves?

Henley and Brooks both confessed their roles in Corll's crimes and led police to most of the bodies. By July 1974, when Henley was convicted in six of the murders and sentenced to six life terms in prison, 21 victims had been identified. Brooks was convicted of one murder, and also sentenced to life. Today, both are at or nearing age 60, memories fading.

Back then, both scribbled extraordinary and lengthy written confessions the day after Henley shot Corll. They contained names, dates, and grisly details of the tortures and deaths, although their gaps left mysteries that the cops didn't yet know would survive most of them. Just one fragment of Henley's confession illustrated the chilling complexities that would face the investigators, families, and eventually, Sharon Derrick:

> *Dean told me about one named Ruben Haney that he killed and buried on the beach at High Island. I shot and killed Johnny Delone, and we buried him at High Island. Then me*

> *and Dean and David Brooks killed two brothers, I think we choked them, anyway, we buried Billy Baulch at High Island and Mike Baulch at Rayburn. We choked Mark Scott and Frank Aguirre and buried them at High Island. The last one I can remember the name of is Homer Garcia, and I shot him in the head and we buried him at Rayburn. I don't remember the dates on all of these, because there has been too many of them. Some of them were hitch-hikers and I don't remember their names. Dean told me that there was 24 in all, but I wasn't with him on all of them.*

So by the end of 2008—two years after Derrick first discovered them in the morgue cooler—three of Corll's victims remained unidentified: ML73-3378. ML73-3349. ML73-3356.

But time had speeded up. The window for finding family members was rapidly closing. Families and memories were dying out, and with them, the chances of putting names to those grim numbers.

"Their families need to know," Derrick told a reporter as she ramped up her efforts to solve the mysteries in 2008. "If there's an 80-year-old mother who has thought, 'Well, maybe my son just didn't love me and just took off and never wanted to see me again,' I would want her to know that he would have come home, that it wasn't his fault he didn't come home."

Derrick met with both of Corll's former teenage accomplices Henley and Brooks in prison. Their memories were still crystal clear and they wanted to help, but they simply didn't recall every little detail that could help her identify the last three lost boys.

Over the years, various labs had been unable to get DNA from the bones. But in 2007, the University of North Texas' Center for Human Identification finally extracted mitochondrial DNA from the bones. With a new DNA profile from the unidentified remains, Derrick sought computerized facial reconstructions.

Then she got a break.

During a routine prison visit with David Brooks, the killer paused ever-so-briefly over the digital reconstruction of ML73-3349. He looked familiar. He couldn't remember the boy's name, but he recalled quite clearly that he'd been shot in the head with a .22-caliber weapon while restrained on Corll's torture board.

What Derrick knew from examining the boy's bones: he'd been shot through the eye with a .22 and had a nylon cord wrapped around his neck.

Derrick played a hunch. She sorted through her missing-person reports from the time of the killings and found one that had possibilities: Randell Lee Harvey, the brother they called Randy.

On March 9, 1971, 15-year-old Randy rode his bike from his Heights home to work at a Fina gas station about three miles away. He was a tall, skinny kid who wore bell-bottom jeans and loved Hendrix, Iron Butterfly and Joplin. He ended his shift and disappeared. His mother reported him missing two days later.

Over the years, Randy's sisters had often tried to share their suspicions with the Houston medical examiner, but were always turned away. They begged their mother to submit DNA, just to see if it matched any of the unidentified victims, but she refused. She thought Randy was long gone, never coming home, and she couldn't bear the thought of officially confirming it.

In 2008, Derrick tracked down two surviving sisters, now in their 50s. One of them bore a striking resemblance to the boy's digital reconstruction. They both recognized a lock of his hair and a blue work jacket found with his body. More importantly, they told Derrick that Randy often wore boots and carried an orange pocket comb remarkably similar to the boots and comb recovered with his remains.

Chillingly, they also told Derrick their brother knew David Brooks. In fact, after Harvey's disappearance, a tipster told police that David Brooks might have killed him in an argument about a stolen stereo, but cops never followed up. One of the sisters had even dated a kid named Malley Winkle, who'd also gone missing around the same time—and later was proven to be one of Corll's victims.

Just before Halloween 2008, armed with that circumstantial evidence and newly extracted DNA from both the boy's corpse and DNA from the two sisters, Derrick confirmed that ML73-3349 was Randell Lee Harvey.

The sisters' grief, bottled up for almost 40 years, tumbled out. But they were also relieved. Eventually, they scattered Randy's ashes at Lake Livingston, where they'd also scattered their mother's ashes in 1994, closing their afternoon service with one of his favorite songs, the Zombies' 1968 hit, "Time of the Season." Derrick gave Randy's sisters a grim but hopeful memento: The peace symbol that had been stitched onto the T-shirt he was wearing the night he was murdered, and they were soothed.

One down. Two to go.

Back in 1973, as the corpses of 27 boys were exhumed from the rented boat shed, the High Island beach, and the woods near Lake Sam Rayburn, investigators did the best they could to identify them. Long before DNA profiling, the identification of decomposed human bodies was more circumstantial than scientific, although medical examiners had some dental records and broken-bone X-rays. Brooks and Henley led diggers to the clandestine graves, often recalling facts about the boys and their deaths as they watched rotting cadavers being dug up.

In 1973, pathology and anthropology collided in a messy way. Autopsists and investigators were more comfortable with fleshy bodies than bones. Bones all looked the same and got the same treatment. The exams were so haphazard that not every body was X-rayed.

The clothing, shoes, and other personal effects unearthed with the bodies were often set aside separately, unassociated with any particular body. A pile of the stuff collected from the boat shed was simply dumped in a box.

"There is a real possibility some of the bodies will never be identified," the Houston medical examiner said just a few days after the horrors were revealed in 1973. Autopsy reports were rushed, sketchy.

Indeed, mistakes were made.

Brooks and Henley's memories, although vivid, weren't perfect. Their separate relationships with Corll were turbulent and inconsistent. They didn't always work together; one might have witnessed a killing and burial, while the other did not   and vice versa.

It was messy work. The corpses were in bad shape, not much more than skeletons with patches of flesh. They relied heavily on physical descriptions of the living boys, but even that was imperfect.

The number of teenage boys who had vanished from their Houston homes and fit the profile of Corll's victims was over 200. By the end of the first week, when the digging suddenly stopped, only 11 of the 27 corpses had been identified, and Houston cops were also eager to wrap up their macabre work quickly.

A year later, five corpses were still unidentified, and all went into the medical examiner's cooler.

In 1985—13 years after he died—the remains of Willard "Rusty" Branch, Jr., the 17-year-old son of a Houston Police officer, were officially identified. Young Branch's father had died of a heart attack while searching for him in 1972, not knowing that his son had already been tortured, emasculated, and shot by Dean Corll before being buried in the boat shed. He was the first victim Henley had brought to Corll, earning himself a $200 "finder's fee."

In 1994, the medical examiner officially identified another lost boy. Only a couple months after Branch's death, Henley and Brooks had abducted a 17-year-old friend named Mark Scott, who fought viciously as they tried to strap him to Corll's torture plank. He was eventually raped and tortured at gunpoint, then strangled before being dumped in the mass grave at High Island.

But in 2011, DNA proved the body was not Scott, but Steven Sickman, whose name had not yet appeared on any list of Corll's potential victims.

Suddenly, a labyrinthine case grew even more complicated.

But until now, Derrick never considered that past identifications might be wrong.

After Derrick identified Randy Harvey in 2008, two sets of unidentified remains from the Corll case sat in the morgue cooler. Both weighed heavily on her. Could at least two of the *identified* victims have been similarly misidentified?

In 2010, an author working on a book about Corll's

crimes shared an eerie suspicion with Derrick about one of the identified victims, Michael Baulch, one of two brothers killed by Corll. The writer noticed that the extent of decomposition and police reports didn't match up. The skeleton hinted at a date of death in August 1972, but the family's missing-persons report was filed almost a year later, after Michael failed to return from a haircut.

Michael's distraught family was shown the grotesque remains in 1973 and although they had some reservations, they identified them as their son.

So Derrick hunted down a surviving sibling and got a DNA sample that confirmed ML73-3378 was, in fact, Michael Baulch.

And the body mistakenly buried with his brother in 1973? DNA analysis confirmed it was Roy Eugene Bunton, a Heights teen last seen by his family leaving for his job at a Houston shoe store in 1972.

And then there was one.

Corll's heinous crimes were dubbed "the Houston Mass Murders," simply because at that time, "mass murder" was the catch-all term for any multiple killing. But soon after Corll's death in 1973, the term "serial killer" was introduced into our lexicon, probably by pioneering FBI profiler Robert Ressler, who saw a powerful, repetitive, psychological cycle within some murderers' behavior—something quite different from the mass-murderers who explode in a single bloody burst. Their motivations, obsessions, and triggers were very different. Corll's case provided a fresh, horrific model for a whole new class of monsters: *serial killers.*

With 29 confirmed victims ranging from age 13 to 21, Corll was officially America's most prolific serial killer for five years, until his body count was surpassed by John

Wayne Gacy's 33 victims in 1978. And Corll's body count is likely much bigger. His accomplices insisted there were at least three more young victims still unfound.

Houston police were widely criticized for abandoning their investigation when Corll's body count exceeded California serial killer Juan Corona's wicked record of 25. They seemed more interested in setting a macabre new record of homicide than truly solving every possible killing by Corll.

But Corll somehow escaped the infamy of the most prolific psychopaths of his day—Manson, Corona, Gacy, Bundy, among them—who've launched a thousand crime books, movies, and TV programs. His name is not among our most recognizable or chilling, even though the sheer monstrosity of his crimes exceeds most of them. Why?

First, his victims.

In the early 1970s, a million kids disappeared from home every year in America. Many were rebels without causes, abandoning their families to seek god-knows-what on the road. Some crashed in communes and cults. Some lived on the streets of San Francisco or Los Angeles. Some took new names and started new lives. They didn't want to be found, like deliberately invisible needles in a windblown haystack. Over the years, some wandered home again. Some didn't.

In Houston, some embarrassed and angry parents didn't even report their teenagers missing, assuming they'd simply joined the mass of unrooted youths in the backwash of the cultural upheaval of the early 1970s.

Houston police wrote off the rest of these boys as delinquents, junkies and hippie kids headed out to California. Most were simple missing-persons cases, since none had turned up dead. In Texas, it wasn't a crime to run away and cops had more pressing issues. Indifferent cops shuffled them off and didn't put a lot of effort into finding them.

Just calling them runaways reduced them somehow.

When the horror finally burst out, the homosexual nature of the crimes and the criminals drove it into darker corners. People began to speak of the victims as if they'd willingly put themselves in a pervert's sights, as if they'd asked to be raped, tortured, and slain   as if, somehow, they'd deserved it. The perception that homosexuality and pedophilia were related made it all seem too sordid to contemplate   so people didn't.

Even before all the decomposing bodies had been unearthed from shallow graves in the boat stall and High Island, some Houstonians rose up against straw men. Homosexuals, pot-smokers, long-hairs, anarchists, and other indistinct bogeymen that had nothing to do with Dean Corll's atrocities.

As a result, attention was almost immediately diverted from a sado-sexual psychopath named Dean Corll, who had killed more humans—in this case, all of them teenage boys—than any American serial killer to that time.

Ironically, because Corll had been honorably discharged from the U.S. Army, his grave in Grand View Memorial Park in Pasadena, Texas, is decorated on every veterans holiday with a little American flag.

How odd that society would remember Dean Corll's service, as brief and unremarkable as it was, but his greater evil has largely escaped our consciousness.

Only one of Corll's known victims remains unidentified today.

His only name, for now, is ML73-3356.

For decades, his bones sat in a plastic tub in the medical examiner's cooler. Then he was moved to an acid-free cardboard body box in the "long-term" cooler where anonymous bones awaited future science. A few years ago, his remains were finally buried in the pauper's field of a county cemetery beneath a simple marker: Unknown 67.

Dr. Sharon Derrick attended the burial along with the family of another Corll victim. For now, she's all the family he has.

He was young, possibly 16. His corpse was already badly decomposed when it was found in a shallow grave near the front of the boat shed, so investigators think he was killed in the late summer or early fall of 1971, but nobody can be sure.

He wore striped Catalina swim trunks with a "C" on the buckle, size 10½ or 11 cowboy boots, and a khaki, long-sleeved shirt with a peace symbol on the back. A simple leather thong had been knotted around his ankle.

Somebody had scrawled a handwritten inscription on his shirt: "LB4MF," "LBHMF," or "L84MF" over the letters "USMC." It made Derrick wonder if the boy had a relative in the service. Something about his clothing made her think he was either protesting the Vietnam war or had some connection to the military. A brother? A father?

He stood 5-foot-5, or maybe 5-foot-6, and his dark brown hair wasn't long, but draped over the tops of his ears. His teeth were in good condition and had no fillings.

The boy appears to have had some kind of developmental problems with his lower spine, maybe spina bifida, that would not have been visible to the casual observer but might have caused him to complain about pain occasionally.

Derrick thinks his name might be Harman, Harmon, or

French, because those are the only names in Houston's missing-persons reports between 1970 and 1973 that fit ML73-3356's physical traits—and almost all of Corll's victims were local. But, sadly, she also knows it's still possible that this lost boy was never reported missing or he drifted through Houston from someplace else.

The boy's DNA profile has been compared against six or seven local families with no match. Now it sits in a national database, waiting for a match that might never come.

Many of the lost boys' parents have died or moved away, or simply moved on. Some don't know   or want to know what became of their children. Some don't want to think their loved ones' lives ended in such phantasmic ways; they might never have imagined their brother or son was slaughtered by a sadistic, homosexual psychopath. Corll's case never became the national phenomenon of other mass killings, and even in the Internet Age, hasn't gotten the wide exposure that might be needed to connect the right dots in time and space. Some have just stopped hoping for their boys to come home.

There are the families who come forward, still seeking after almost 50 years, some signs of life   or proof of death in boys they haven't seen since Nixon was president. They might be dead, or alive, or just forever disconnected. Boys whose names are on no lists, no police reports, no death certificates. For most of them, there are no answers.

In 2012, another macabre artifact surfaced: A chilling Polaroid of a handcuffed teenage boy was found among Henley's possessions. The blurry image showed a terrified young boy hunched over on the floor, wearing handcuffs near a toolbox that was found after Corll's murder in 1973. When Henley was shown the Polaroid in prison, he didn't recall the boy, but repeated there were other victims who've never been found. This new one doesn't match the profile of any known victims. Is he the 29th lost boy? Will his body—nevermind his name and face—ever be found?

And who knows how many other moldering, tortured corpses of young boys lie unfound in hidden graves in Southeast Texas? Almost certainly, some remain. Almost certainly, some families might never know what became of their sons and brothers, whose flesh and bones are slowly and secretly decaying into the Texas dirt someplace.

So Sharon Derrick waits, hoping there aren't any more while fearing there are.

She can't let go.

Dr. Sharon Derrick

Do you know this boy?

ML73-3356
See more at
https://identifyus.org/cases/4547

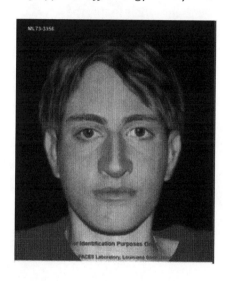

The skeletal remains of this white male, age 15-19, were found August 9, 1973, in a shallow grave inside a boat-storage unit rented by serial killer Dean Corll. They have never been identified.

He was about 5-foot-5 or 5-foot-6. He had brown hair. His teeth were in good condition and had no fillings.

He wore a khaki, long-sleeved shirt with a peace sign and the hand-written letters "USMC" and "L84MF" (or maybe "LBHMF," or "L84MF"). He also had dark blue corduroy pants (size 32x30) over brightly striped swim trunks. He had size 10½ or 11 cowboy boots, and a khaki, long-sleeved shirt with a peace symbol on the back. A simple leather thong had been knotted around his ankle.

It's possible (though not certain) that he disappeared in the Houston area in the late summer or fall of 1971. He might not have been a Houston resident, but odds are that he was from the region.

The boy appears to have suffered some developmental problems with his lower spine, maybe spina bifida, that would not have been visible to the casual observer but might have resulted in him occasionally complaining about pain.

If you have information, please contact Dr. Sharon Derrick, Harris County (TX) Institute of Forensic Sciences at 713-796-6858.

The Darkest Tower

University of Texas Tower massacre
August 1, 1966

Roland 'Cap' Ehlke in Austin

A midsummer thunderstorm was brewing to the west. A warm mist had settled over Milwaukee.

Rev. Roland Ehlke rolled up his car window against the sultry air and listened to the radio as he drove on his afternoon hospital rounds.

Then a newscaster broke in with a bulletin about a sniper who was killing people from a perch in a tower high above the University of Texas campus in Austin.

Rev. Ehlke turned up the volume and listened closely. After all, his twenty-one-year-old middle son Cap was on the UT campus, being trained for a Peace Corps job overseas.

"But it's a big campus," the pastor silently reassured himself. "He won't be involved in this."

Later, the newscaster came back with more details about the unfolding tragedy in Texas. And again, Rev. Ehlke thought about his Cap. He was a little disappointed that Cap, who'd recently graduated from a Lutheran college, had skipped going directly to seminary and decided instead to go adventuring. When Cap joined the Peace Corps and got assigned to teach English to Iranian kids, he couldn't exactly find Iran on the globe, but he didn't care. He was going to see the world.

The Peace Corps had sent him to Austin for the summer with other volunteers to learn basic Farsi, Iranian customs and Muslim culture.

Now the world was watching as a madman with a high-powered rifle sprayed the college with bullets from a lofty tower.

" many people have reportedly been wounded," the man on the radio said, "and some are dead ..."

Misty rain clabbered on the Ford's windshield. Cap was a fresh-faced Midwestern boy from Wisconsin, his father reasoned. The son of a preacher knew how to detour around trouble. And Austin was a big enough city. What were the chances? Good kids didn't just find themselves in the crosshairs of lunatics.

"Cap wouldn't be involved," the Rev. Ehlke told himself.

Twelve hundred miles away, Cap was involved.

By the long, hot summer of 1966, the simmering fever of Americans' unrest with the war in Vietnam, with the status of women and blacks, with the old sexual ethos, with the establishment—with almost everything that represented the previous generation's sensibilities—had exploded into a furious furnace of violence and disorder. Time had inexplicably speeded up. The world was in upheaval. Wars raged between nations, races, sexes, faiths, young and old, fathers and sons.

It seemed like everything was falling apart that summer. A president had been assassinated less than three years before. Race riots were erupting in major cities. More American soldiers were dying than South Vietnamese in "their" war. Armed troops and demonstrators were squaring off in the street. Draft cards and bras were being burned in spectacular fires of discontent. The sexual revolution was redefining relationships between men and women, while sowing seeds that would rock the rest of the century. Professors were encouraging their students to use psychedelic drugs. A new kind of book about mass murder, Truman Capote's *In Cold Blood*, became an instant bestseller. And a homeless ex-con named Richard Speck raped, stabbed, and strangled eight student nurses in Chicago in one of the most horrifying American crimes ever committed.

There were a lot of ways to get hurt in those days of rage. Some people simply went mad.

And college campuses were among the most dangerous of danger zones. The ivory towers and tree-lined quads had become incubators for protest, radicalism, and experimentation.

Yet the national unrest had pretty much skipped the University of Texas. Maybe because Austin was a tiny island floating in a sea of more conservative values than Berkeley, Rutgers, or even UW-Madison. Or maybe because Austin already had the reputation of going against the grain. But outside of minor incidents of civil disobedience, mostly over race issues during the civil rights movement, the UT campus had so far been spared the roiling turbulence of the 1960s. So far.

Cap Ehlke was just a Midwestern preacher's kid, as white and impressionable as a fresh sheet of paper. Born of good German stock in the tiny lakeside village of Two Rivers, Wisconsin, he had grown up in a middle-class neighborhood on Milwaukee's south side where his father pastored a Lutheran church. A soft-spoken kid, he loved school, played intramural tennis, dated a few girls casually and stayed out of trouble. His parents always hoped he'd go into the ministry someday.

After graduating from a prep school, Cap entered Northwestern College, a small school established at the end of the Civil War in Watertown, Wisconsin, to train Lutheran pastors. Most of Cap's classmates intended to graduate and continue their theological studies to be ordained as ministers, but by the time he graduated in 1966, Cap had different ideas.

It wasn't that he didn't wish to be a pastor. He just wanted something else more. Or first. Or for now. He didn't even know what it was. He couldn't give it name or point to it on a map. He just knew it wasn't the cloistered life of a Wisconsin seminarian on a long slide into the life of a Wisconsin clergyman in a cold Wisconsin village.

He let it be known that after graduation, he'd be joining the Peace Corps, a fledgling army of young American volunteers dispatched to the most desperate corners of the earth to put a human face on the United States as they lent a helping hand. By 1966, a record 15,000 volunteers—almost all idealistic young students—were digging wells, teaching school, harvesting crops, and administering medicine throughout the Third World.

The president of Northwestern himself tried to talk Cap out of it. He said the ministry was more important, that he could affect far more lives as a pastor than by spending a couple years on the other side of a troubled world. Besides, he reminded Cap that he might have to repay Wisconsin's Lutherans for his "free" education if he didn't take the next logical step into seminary in the fall.

But Cap stood his ground, shaky as it was. The next chapter in his young life would be an adventure, not more books and Wisconsin winters. When the Peace Corps assigned him to teach English to Iranian children, he consulted an atlas to see where exactly in the world Iran was located. After a summer training course at the University of Texas, he'd ship out in the fall to begin his two-year tour of duty in a place he didn't know, far away from the only place he knew.

Next stop: Austin.

Charles Whitman

Charlie Whitman was an enigma wrapped in a man-child. An Eagle Scout and altar boy with a high IQ, his family could afford the better things in life. Charlie learned to play the piano very young, took up a paper route, and learned to shoot so well that his proud father once crowed, "Charlie could plug a squirrel in the eye by the time he was sixteen." Outgoing and ambitious, he grew up to be a popular athlete and model student at his parochial high school in Florida, where he graduated seventh in his Class of 1959.

But Charlie had a tense relationship with his domineering, abusive father who demanded perfection from his wife and children—and beat them when they disappointed him. Just before his eighteenth birthday, when he came home from a party drunk, his father beat him fiercely and threw him into the swimming pool, where he nearly drowned. It was the last straw for Charlie, who enlisted in the U.S. Marine Corps a few days later. He wanted nothing more obsessively than to be better and smarter than his cruel, semi-literate father. That would show him.

Early on, he thrived in the Corps, as he had under his father's authoritarian watch. With his blond crew cut and skinny frame, he might not have looked the part of a leatherneck, but he developed into a good one on active duty in Guantanamo Bay, Cuba, one of the world's Cold War hotspots. Qualified as a sharpshooter, he excelled at rapid-fire marksmanship, especially with moving targets.

In fact, Whitman was such a good Marine that he won a special military scholarship to study engineering and set himself on track to become a commissioned officer. In the fall of 1961, Whitman enrolled at the University of Texas in Austin and declared his major in mechanical engineering, still a Marine but beyond the daily control of his superiors.

Without the rigid discipline he'd known for his whole life, it was a disaster. Whitman's grades tanked. He gave up studying for gambling and began wearing a .357 handgun under his shirt, ostensibly as protection against enemies he made in his late-night, high-stakes poker games.

One night, Whitman sat on the balcony of his dorm room, peering across the campus at the 307-foot Tower, a Spanish colonial that stood at the dead-center of the sprawling campus. Austin's tallest building—even taller than the nearby state capitol dome—the Tower was the city's first skyscraper when it was built in 1937. Rallies and debates take place on its steps, and it looms over all graduation ceremonies. Deep inside are twenty tons of bells, and its limestone walls were regularly swathed in orange floodlights after major sports victories.

The Tower was not just the most visible symbol of the

University of Texas, it was its beating heart.

"A person could stand off an Army before they got to him up there," the Marine sharpshooter mused. He'd love to shoot people from up there, he said to nobody in particular. But nobody took him seriously. After all, Charlie was a good soldier, a mature guy, and a joker at heart. He couldn't be serious.

In February 1962, Whitman was introduced to a freshman coed named Kathy Leissner who was studying to be a teacher. After a starry-eyed courtship, they married six months later.

If marriage improved Whitman's attitude, it didn't improve his grades. A semester after the wedding, the Marine Corps withdrew his scholarship and ordered him back to active duty at Camp Lejeune, North Carolina, while Kathy stayed in Austin to finish her education.

The return to regimented military life was claustrophobic. No longer a good soldier, Whitman rebelled. He was court-martialed for gambling and busted back to the rank of private. Desperate to get out, he turned to an unlikely ally, his father, who used his political connections to cut Charlie's enlistment. Charles Whitman was honorably discharged in December 1964 and returned to Austin, where he re-enrolled at UT in the spring of 1965. His new major: architectural engineering.

He took a part-time bank teller's job for $1.25 an hour and worked as a scout master in his spare time. But he wrote secretly in his journals with a darkening hand about his lack of self-esteem, expressing frustration with the dysfunctions in his family, blaming himself for his problems, and meticulously listing ways he could be a better husband. He hated that Kathy was a better breadwinner than he, and he was ashamed for accepting money from his father. He feared something was wrong inside his brain and that he was sterile. He openly declared he didn't believe in God anymore. He began to see himself as an All-American loser.

Whitman didn't know what a happy marriage looked like; his own father and mother had been poor examples. As a result, if his spirit was willing to try to be a better husband, his flesh had no idea how a good husband behaves.

And he behaved badly. He was a perfectionist like his father, and he began almost from the beginning to expect more of Kathy than she could give. He would check for dust *behind* picture frames and talk about his sex life with friends while Kathy was in the room. He hit her on at least three separate occasions during their marriage, and his journals reflected his regrets over being too harsh with her.

It grew worse when his parents divorced in the spring of 1966 and his mother Margaret moved from Florida to Austin to be near her son. She rented an apartment near downtown, not far from Charlie and Kathy's modest, five-room bungalow at 906 Jewell Street.

Worse, Whitman's abuse of amphetamines, especially Dexedrine, had gotten out of control. He needed the pills to stay awake, but friends recall him tossing them back "like popcorn." During finals week, he reportedly stayed awake for five days and nights, slept over the weekend, and did it again—nearly two weeks hopped up on chemicals and without restorative sleep. He was also taking other drugs—some legal and some not—to combat the effects of the amphetamines and to deal with his depression and stress. His medicine cabinet at home contained thirteen different pill bottles prescribed by seven different doctors.

Kathy saw her husband's turmoil. She begged him to get

counseling, but he resisted. When his parents divorced in the spring of 1966, he was suffering from severe headaches, and so he finally visited a university psychiatrist.

He told the doctor how much he hated his father. He lamented what a failure he'd become. He even mentioned how he had fantasized about "going up on the Tower with a deer rifle and shooting people."

Although the shrink noted that Whitman "seemed to be oozing with hostility," he wasn't particularly alarmed. First, he saw Whitman as a man who had basically good values. Second, he'd been listening to troubled, suicidal students fantasize about the Tower for years, and it no longer startled him. The doctor concluded Whitman was unlikely to hurt himself or anyone else and asked him to come back in a week for another session.

Charles Whitman never returned.

July 31, 1966, was a Sunday, and it dawned Texas hot. It would reach 101°F that day, the hottest day of the year so far. That morning, Charlie drove Kathy to her summer job at Southwestern Bell, where she was working a split shift.

After he dropped Kathy at her downtown office, Charlie paid cash for some Spam and small food items at a convenience store, then bought a Bowie knife and a pair of binoculars at an Army surplus store for $18.98.

At 1 p.m., he picked up Kathy and they went to a movie followed by a late lunch with his mother Margaret. They killed more time before Kathy had to go back for the late half of her shift by visiting friends, who later remembered Charlie as being unusually quiet.

At 6 p.m. he dropped Kathy back at work and went home to Jewell Street. Alone in the little house where he and his wife had so recently talked about having children,

Charles Whitman went to the back bedroom, calmly rolled a sheet of paper into his typewriter and began to explain as best he could why he was about to become a mass murderer.

> Sunday,
> July 31, 1966
> 6:45 P.M.
> I don't quite understand what it is that compels me to type this letter. Perhaps it is to leave some vague reason for the actions I have recently performed. [Author's note: Whitman had not actually yet performed these "actions" but was writing this note to be found after he had.] I don't really understand myself these days. I am supposed to be an average reasonable and intelligent young man. However, lately (I can't recall when it started) I have been a victim of many unusual and irrational thoughts. These thoughts constantly recur and it requires a tremendous mental effort to concentrate on useful and progressive tasks. In March when my parents made a physical break I noticed a great deal of stress. I consulted a Dr. Cochrum at the University Health Center and asked him to recommend someone that I could consult with about some psychiatric disorders I felt I had. I talked with a Doctor once for about two hours and tried to convey to him my fears that I felt some overwhelming violent impulses. After one session I never saw the Doctor again, and since then I have been fighting my mental turmoil alone, and seemingly to no avail.
> After my death I wish that an autopsy would be performed on me to see if there is any visible physical disorder. I have had some tremendous

headaches in the past and have consumed two large bottles of Excedrin in the past three months.

It was after much thought that I decided to kill my wife, Kathy, tonight after I pick her up from work at the telephone company. I love her dearly, and she has been as fine a wife to me as any man could ever hope to have. I cannot rationally pinpoint any specific reason for doing this. I don't know whether it is selfishness, or if I don't want her to have to face the embarrassment my actions would surely cause her. At this time, though, the prominent reason in my mind is that I truly do not consider this world worth living in, and am prepared to die, and I do not want to leave her to suffer alone in it. I intend to kill her as painlessly as possible.

Similar reasons provoked me to take my mother's life also. I don't think the poor woman has ever enjoyed life as she is entitled to. She was a simple young woman who married a very possessive and dominating man. All my life as a boy until I ran away from home to join the Marine Corps

A knock at the door interrupted him. It was another couple, best friends of the Whitmans, dropping in for a Sunday visit. Rather than shooing them away, Charlie invited them in.

They talked for an hour or so about everything and nothing—the Vietnam war, upcoming exams, Charlie's dream of buying some land near the Guadalupe River. Charlie seemed upbeat to them, talking about Kathy with more affection that he normally did. The pleasant visit came to a happy end around 8:30 p.m. when an ice cream truck passed and they all ran outside to flag it down. The ice cream tasted good because it had been a hot day and the night was not cooling off.

A little after 9:30 p.m., Charlie picked up Kathy in their new black Chevy Impala and took her home. The night was uncommonly hot and the Jewell Street house had no air-conditioning, so Charlie asked his mother if he and Kathy could come to her air-conditioned apartment to cool off before bed. Kathy begged off, but a little before midnight, Charlie drove over to Margaret's flat, while Kathy slipped naked into bed, hoping for the slightest Texas breeze through their little bedroom window.

Margaret met Charlie in the high-rise's lobby around midnight and escorted him up to her fifth-floor apartment. Alone inside, he strangled her with a piece of rubber hose before stabbing her in the chest with a hunting knife and either shooting her or bashing the back of her head violently. He also smashed her left hand with such force that the diamond flew out of her wedding ring, which became embedded in the ruined flesh of her finger. She was only forty-three.

He then sat down with a yellow legal pad and wrote another letter, explaining that he had killed his mother to relieve her suffering at the hands of her husband. He lifted her corpse onto her bed, covered her wounds with the bedspread, and laid the letter neatly upon her. A little after 2 a.m., he returned to the Jewell Street house, where Kathy slept peacefully.

Standing over her in the darkness, he plunged his Bowie knife into her naked chest five times, hitting her heart and killing her instantly. He pulled the blankets over her and washed his hands before he returned to the unfinished letter he'd begun hours before. In his own handwriting—not typing, as he had begun the letter—he scrawled in the margin:

*friends
interrupted
8-1-66
Mon
3:00 A.M.
Both Dead*

I was a witness to her being beaten at least once a month. Then when she took enough my father wanted to fight to keep her below her usual standard of living.

I imagine it appears that I bruttaly [sic] kill both of my loved ones. I was only trying to do a quick thorough job.

If my life insurance policy is valid, please see that all the worthless checks I wrote this weekend are made good. Please pay off my debts. I am 25 years old and have been financially independent.

Donate the rest anonymously to a mental health foundation. Maybe research can prevent further tragedies of this type.

Charles J. Whitman

If you can find it in yourself to grant my last wish Cremate me after the autopsy.

Not once did he mention the horror he was about to visit upon a city and a nation. He spent the rest of the night re-reading his journals, writing goodbye notes to others, and gathering the supplies he needed for the daylight, just a few hours away. Many items that he packed in his old Marine footlocker spoke more of survival than death: a radio, a blank notebook, jugs of water and gasoline, Spam and other food, deodorant, toilet paper, several knives and a hatchet, ropes, a compass, an alarm clock, a flashlight and batteries, a machete, several gun scabbards, matches, and various pieces of hunting equipment. He expected a long siege.

But some of it spoke of death, too. After the sun rose on another hot Texas day, he visited at least three Austin stores where he bought more guns and ammunition and a dolly to wheel his deadly arsenal, which now included a high-powered 6mm Remington rifle with a scope, two other hunting rifles, a sawed-off shotgun, three pistols, the large hunting knife he'd already used to kill his wife and mother, and an astounding 700 rounds of ammo.

He dressed in sneakers, jeans, and a plaid shirt under blue nylon overalls, trying to disguise himself as an inconspicuous workman hauling a dolly of equipment.

He scrawled a last note and left it in the house: "*8-1-66. I never could quite make it. These thoughts are too much for me.*"

A little past 11 a.m., Charles Whitman closed the front door of the little bungalow on Jewell Street for the last time, loaded his footlocker in his car, and drove away toward the University of Texas campus.

Cap Ehlke sat in a Peace Corps training class, watching the clock tick toward lunch. For more than a month, the preparatory classes had been droning on. It was intense, but not much different from regular college work. He was eager to get into the field and see the world, and another month of classes seemed more like an obstacle than a necessity.

Most days, he and some of his Peace Corps classmates would grab a quick lunch on "the Drag," as UT students called Guadalupe Street, a noisy thoroughfare that cut across the western edge of campus where many cafes and shops catered to the kids. Cap loved the college hangouts and the different people he met.

When class finally let out at noon, Cap and two friends, Dave Mattson and Tom Herman, started a long, hot walk to a school cafeteria, where they planned to meet a new friend, Thomas Ashton, for lunch. All four were headed to Iran in the fall.

The heat was oppressive and the humid air still as death as they walked three abreast down Guadalupe. Road workers were fixing the street, and the lunchtime traffic was heavier than usual. Kids passed them on the sidewalk, where Vietnam appeared on most of the front pages in the newsstands, and many passing girls were wearing their hair long and straight. Cap noticed both.

As they passed traffic barricades in front of Sheftall's Jewelry, a little shop beside the university bookstore, Cap heard several pops. Firecrackers, he thought. Or road workers with an air hammer, or maybe a stupid fraternity prank.

Beside him, Dave shrieked. Cap looked down to see Dave cupping his right hand in his left. It was nearly severed from his wrist, bleeding profusely. *What the hell?* he thought. *Didn't they know that firecrackers can hurt people?*

Then he noticed the left sleeve of his madras shirt was riddled with small holes and flecked with blood, and it made him angrier.

Suddenly, his upper right arm was jolted, as if he'd been punched by someone unseen. A deep gash in his triceps began to pour blood into his shredded sleeve.

"Take cover!" somebody yelled down the street.

Cap and Tom, who wasn't wounded, hunkered near the wall of the bookstore, but Dave simply crumpled in shock on the sidewalk, holding his dismembered hand and muttering to himself. People were running all around them, taking cover. Cap thought he saw a girl's lifeless body lying on the pavement up the street. His arm wounds were starting to burn.

Nobody knew what was happening. He heard more distant pops but there was so much confusion, and Dave needed help.

"We've got to get off the sidewalk," he hollered.

Cap and Tom left their hiding place and crawled to Dave. Together they dragged him across the hot concrete to the jewelry store's front door, just a few feet away. Little pings and puffs of dust erupted all around them as the mysterious, distant pops continued.

Jewelry store manager Homer Kelley saw kids crawling around on the sidewalk and was suspicious of a college prank—until he saw the blood. As the sixty-four-year-old Kelley ran outside to help drag the boys to safety, something hit him in the lower left leg.

Inside, Cap collapsed on the ripped carpet with Dave, still stunned. All around him, more than a dozen other people hid behind display cases and furniture as broken glass flew from the front windows. Some were also wounded. One man lay bleeding from his belly while others made bandages from handkerchiefs.

Cap could hear gunshots behind the store. It slowly dawned on him that they'd been hit by bullets fired in front of the store, and they continued to fly from the opposite direction. It made him think they were caught in the crossfire of a spectacular gunfight, or maybe a jewelry store robbery.

The frightened people around him were coming to the same fearful conclusion.

"It's a whole gang out there," somebody said. "They're coming in here!"

Then Cap noticed that the left thigh of his tan jeans was perforated with tiny holes, and blood welled up in a widening stain. He had been wounded three times. He didn't know his friend Thomas Ashton, who the three boys were on their way to meet, was already dead. And he didn't know why anyone would shoot at him.

There was no reason. There was no gang. There was no robbery.

Just one berserk killer in a tower.

Pretending to be a janitor, Charles Whitman had wheeled his arsenal into the University of Texas Tower, killing three innocent people there before barricading himself on the tower's observation deck.

At 1:00 p.m., with his weapons arrayed all around him in his impenetrable fortress, Charlie Whitman took aim at a nine-months pregnant young woman walking with her boyfriend on campus. He hit her in the belly, and as she fell, her boyfriend crouched over her. Charlie shot him, too.

He commenced shooting anyone he could see. He had a 360-degree field of fire, and he proved lethal.

For the next ninety-six minutes, Whitman killed with uncanny precision. He hit some victims up to 500 yards away, and zeroed in on frantic, running bodies with deadly accuracy. Her dropped them all: first, the pregnant freshman and her boyfriend who tried to shield her   then the young math professor   Peace Corps volunteer Thomas Ashton, who was simply walking toward the sound of gun shots   the student running away   the cop who peeked out from his hiding place   the PhD candidate with six kids

the new high school graduate and his girlfriend who dreamed of being a dancer   the city electrical repairman who just wanted to help somebody   the seventeen-year-old girl who attended the same school where Kathy taught

the electrical engineering student who'd take another thirty-five years to die from his wounds

With one hundred fifty bullets, Whitman hit almost fifty people.

All the while, a CBS television crew was filming inside the free-fire zone, and news photographers were risking their lives to snap images for the next day's paper. Citizens all over the city—including Whitman himself—had dialed their transistor radios to listen to the live coverage.

Minutes after the first shot, Austin police scrambled to the scene, where one of them had already been killed. A police sniper was sent aloft in an airplane, but Whitman drove them away with his gunfire. As word spread on the radio, dozens of angry citizens arrived with deer rifles and returned fire at the Tower.

As police slowly moved across the killing ground toward the Tower, they helped the wounded as best they could, even as Whitman continued to fire at ambulances trying to save them.

A handful of policemen finally got to the Tower. Once inside, Officers Ramiro Martinez and Houston McCoy—with the help of a civilian deputized on the scene—crept to the observation deck but found the door wedged shut. When McCoy finally breached the door, they both crept toward the sound of Whitman's shots, even as bullets from the ground ricocheted off the walls around them.

McCoy caught Whitman's eye for a split second, then blasted him in the face with a shotgun. His head flipped back and his body spasmed as McCoy hit him with another blast in the left side of his head. At the same moment, Martinez emptied six shots from his service revolver into Whitman.

He was dead, but McCoy and Martinez ran to his twitching body and each fired a last shot at point-blank range into him. As Whitman's blood drained into a rain gutter near his shattered head, McCoy grabbed a green towel from Whitman's footlocker and waved it to the people on the ground.

The siege was over. At 1:24 p.m., Charles Whitman was dead.

Whitman was likely already dead when Cap and the others hiding in the jewelry store—and most people on the ground—escaped into an alley and scrambled over a wooden fence into the arms of paramedics on the other side. In the alley, Cap saw ordinary people aiming their rifles toward the Tower and a few more pieces of this bloody puzzle fell into place.

Several injured people were already in the ambulance, including the driver himself, who was critically wounded. Morris Hohmann, one of the drivers, was responding to the victims on West Twenty-third Street when one of Whitman's bullets pierced a leg artery. His partner used his belt as a tourniquet and took him to Brackenridge Hospital with the other victims.

At Brackenridge, the dead and wounded were piling up in the city's only full-service emergency room. Chaos reigned in the hospital's hallways, where cops, reporters, and relatives rushed around among the dead and dying. Meanwhile, hundreds of local citizens lined up at Brackenridge and the local blood center to donate.

In the ER, somebody told Cap what had happened: a madman in the Tower had been shooting innocent people, and many were dead.

When a doctor finally saw Cap, he found serious shrapnel wounds in his upper left arm, the front of his left leg, his back, and his left hand—all caused by Whitman's soft-tipped bullets splattering against his friend Dave's wrist bones and the walls and sidewalks of Guadalupe. He'd also been hit directly in the soft flesh of his upper right arm; the bullet furrowed six inches across the meat of his triceps. None were life-threatening, but all had come close to something much more serious.

Brackenridge soon transferred Cap to the University Health Center, where he spent a week recuperating from his wounds, some of which suppurated for months. There, he was told that Thomas Ashton, his Peace Corps buddy, had been killed. And he began to contemplate how close he'd come to death.

Outside his hospital window loomed the Tower. This edifice seemingly within an arm's reach had come to symbolize so many things to so many people, including Charles Whitman. Now it became a symbol of something else to Cap Ehlke: the nearness of death.

"As I lay in the clean, white bed at the clinic, I could look out the window and see that lofty tower," he wrote later. "At night it was lit up. Piercing into the dark sky, it gave me an eerie feeling, as stark as death itself. It made me think about the ultimate meaning of things."

After he was released, Cap joined up with another Peace Corps group that had been sent to Mexico to practice teaching before shipping out to the Middle East. He was assigned to a high school in Mexico City for a few weeks, but he felt out of sync with the group. His wounds weren't healing properly, and he was still obsessed with his brush with death. Or with God.

The shooting had jolted him back into a spiritual focus. He still wanted adventure, but maybe it wasn't as far as Iran or all the other places he never knew. Maybe it was closer than all that.

He picked up the phone and called the seminary. The

new semester had already begun, he was told, but they took him anyway.

The next summer, he went to Iran to visit some of his old Peace Corps friends, including Dave Mattson, whose hand had been reattached by surgeons. He explored Europe that summer, too, before traveling to Jerusalem six weeks after the Six Day War between Israel and Egypt. The air was electric in those days, and it thrilled him.

Later, he attended Hebrew University in Israel before finishing at seminary. He was sent to a small church in Little Chute, Wisconsin, and made a family. He was, at last, the minister his father expected him to be.

In time, he returned to Milwaukee as an editor for a Lutheran publishing house, where he worked for fifteen years. Cap eventually collected four master's degrees and a doctorate, and he took a teaching position at Concordia University, a Lutheran college on the shores of Lake Michigan in Mequon, a northern suburb of Milwaukee.

For many years, he kept the bloodied pants he wore that day in Austin, but they have disappeared. So have some of the memories he thought he'd never forget. Somewhere there's a box full of clippings and mementoes from those dark days, but he has lost track of them. Reading other people's memories might somehow taint his own.

"I just have never looked at my survival as some kind of great accomplishment," he says now. "It was just something I was involved in. In some ways, it seemed kind of morbid to want to revisit it."

He feels no animosity toward Charles Whitman, partly because he never saw it as a personal attack.

"What he did was terrible, and he went over the edge," Cap says. "It was like being hit by lighting, being touched by some force outside of me. I happen to have been shot by him, but my relationship to Charles Whitman is no different than someone's who wasn't even there.

"If anything, it made me aware of how we are always close to death. An inch or two either way can make all the difference."

In ninety-six horrifying minutes, Charles Whitman had killed fourteen people and wounded thirty-one. The discovery of his wife and mother's corpses brought the day's grim toll to sixteen.

A long line of American mass murderers preceded Charlie Whitman, and a longer line came after, but the Texas Tower massacre—possibly because of the iconic tower itself—became an archetype for wholesale slaughter. Or possibly because it would be twenty-two years before another crazed shooter—James Huberty at the San Ysidro McDonald's in 1984—would exceed Whitman's grisly body count.

In the days after the orgiastic slaughter in Austin, an autopsy showed that Whitman had a malignant, walnut-sized tumor deep in his brain, just as he had feared. But doctors concluded that it was unlikely to have caused his rampage, even though they believed it might have killed him within a year. But some scoff at the suggestion that a tumor, drug abuse, insomnia, or anything but raw evil caused Whitman's rampage.

"Charlie Whitman knew precisely and completely what he was doing when he ascended the University of Texas Tower and shot nearly fifty people," wrote Gary Lavergne, whose meticulously detailed book, *A Sniper in the Tower,* stands as the definitive account of the crime. "He could not have done what he did without controlled, thoughtful, serial decision-making in a correct order to accomplish a goal.

Nothing he did remotely appears undisciplined or random.

[He] was a cold and calculating murderer. Those who say they can't believe he would commit such a monstrous crime are only admitting that they didn't really know him."

Charlie Whitman died as he had lived, an enigma.

Ironically, he was buried beside his beloved mother—his first victim—in a Catholic cemetery in Florida. A priest blessed Charlie's gray, flag-draped casket as it was lowered into hallowed ground, saying he had obviously been mentally ill and was therefore not responsible for the sin of murder.

Kathy Leissner Whitman, only twenty-three when her husband stabbed her to death, was buried in Rosenberg, Texas, not far from the little town where she grew up.

As so often has happened after gun crimes, a groundswell of anti-gun hysteria erupted after the tower massacre. But it was stillborn: Charlie Whitman was a military-trained marksman who possessed legal weapons that he legally purchased. He had no previous criminal record and knew more about firearms than most gun owners. As many pointed out at the time, he could have taught the gun-ownership courses that any state might have mandated.

For many, it wasn't what Whitman knew or what he couldn't control that caused his crimes. He was in complete control of his actions and understood their profound consequences.

"Charles Whitman knew that what he was doing was evil," Gary Lavergne concluded in *A Sniper in the Tower*. "[He] became a killer because he did not respect or admire himself. He knew that in many ways he was what he despised in others.

"He wanted to die in a big way   he died while engaging

in the only activity in which he truly excelled: shooting."

For two years after the mass murder, the Tower's observation deck was closed. After it reopened in 1968, a series of suicide leaps forced it to close again in 1974. Finally, after several safety improvements, it reopened in 1999.

Nine years after the killings, when Hollywood proposed a TV movie about the massacre, starring a post-Disney Kurt Russell as Whitman, the University of Texas refused to allow filming at the Tower, saying it would be an affront to the still-raw emotions in Austin. *The Deadly Tower* was eventually filmed at the state capitol building in Baton Rouge, Louisiana, and aired in late 1975 to lukewarm reviews. The movie itself is five minutes shorter than Whitman's real-time shooting spree.

The Tower's symbolism is so potent that for years UT offered a college course, "The UT Tower and Public Memory."

"After more than thirty years of institutional repression and silence," its teacher, Professor Rosa Eberly, wrote in 1999, "UT has been presented with an opportunity to come to terms publicly with one of the most troubling incidents in its history. The university has, at least institutionally, begun to heal and move beyond the violent effects of Charles Whitman's actions in 1966 and the enduring pain of those who witnessed or were otherwise affected by the several suicides there."

Forty years later, in 2006, the university mounted an inconspicuous bronze plaque beside a turtle pond just north of the Tower as a memorial "to those who died, to those who were wounded, and to the countless other victims who were immeasurably affected by the tragedy." This is the only memorial to the massacre on the UT campus.

For a long time, the Tower bore the pockmarks where bullets had hit, but they have all been patched, and the divots are barely noticeable. Today, tower tour guides are instructed not to talk about the Whitman massacre as the university tries to minimize the memory of August 1, 1966. All visitors must first pass through a metal detector at ground level, and an armed guard accompanies all tour groups to the observation deck.

But many people will never forget. Officer Houston McCoy, who suffered from post-traumatic stress for years after he killed Whitman in the Tower, is one.

"If I get to heaven and see Charles Whitman," he once said, "I'm going to have to kill him all over again."

Nightmare at Noon

Luby's Cafeteria Massacre in Killeen, Texas

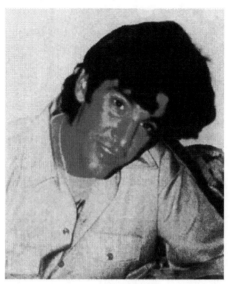

George Hennard

October 16, 1991
Suzanna Gratia really didn't have time for lunch today. She had a dozen errands to run and a full afternoon schedule at her chiropractic clinic in Copperas Cove, Texas. She was just thirty-one, a single woman struggling to build a small business in a small town. She refused to waste a sunny autumn weekday slacking off. She'd already declined a lunch offer from a friend who managed the Luby's Cafeteria

in Killeen, ten miles up U.S. 190. Time was money, and Suzanna needed both.

So when Suzanna's retired parents, Al and Suzy Gratia, dropped in after their Wednesday morning golf game and invited her to lunch, she begged off. After all, she saw them almost every day. They lived next door, and Suzy, a former executive secretary at Boeing in Houston, closely watched the clinic's administrative operations while Al, who'd recently sold his heavy-equipment dealership, kept Suzanna's books.

Less than two weeks ago, the Gratias had celebrated their forty-seventh anniversary at a big family party, but Al and Suzy were anything but fragile geezers waiting to die. Al was seventy-one and Suzy was sixty-seven, but they traveled and golfed most mornings. Al spent his afternoons writing a book and local newspaper columns. Still, they had more time on their hands than Suzanna and today she needed her lunch hour for more pressing things.

So mom and dad bartered for her company: if Suzanna would eat lunch with them, they'd run some of her errands for her.

Suzanna couldn't refuse. She called her buddy, Luby's manager Mark Kopenhaffe, and accepted his offer. On the way, she and her mother dreamed up plans for Al and Suzy's fiftieth anniversary party. When they arrived at Luby's a little after noon, the parking lot was already packed. It was the day after payday at Fort Hood as well as National Boss's Day, and employees around Killeen didn't have too many other choices for a cheap, fast lunch with their supervisors.

Suzanna parked her Mercedes in a side lot. But before she got out, she slipped her Smith & Wesson .38-caliber handgun out of her purse. Soon after she graduated from chiropractic school and moved to Houston, one of her patients—a prosecutor—suggested she carry a gun for protection in the big city, even though concealed weapons were against the law in Texas. "Better to be tried by 12 than carried by six," he joked.

So a friend gave her a gun and taught her to shoot it. She was licensed to carry it, but Texas law forbade her from taking a hidden weapon into a public place. So now, rather than risk losing her hard-won chiropractic license by breaking the law, she tucked the snub-nosed revolver safely out of sight, behind her front passenger seat.

Besides, she only carried a gun for menacing moments, lonely roads, and dark places where young women needed protection from monsters—not crowded family restaurants on warm, sunny days in small central Texas towns.

What Suzanna didn't know is that at the same moment, a young man not much older than she, his head filled with demons and his pockets filled with bullets, was barreling toward a bloody cataclysm the world never saw coming.

George Hennard was an unfinished soul.

Born October 15, 1956, in Pennsylvania, this son of an authoritarian Army surgeon father and a doting, narcissistic mother grew up a loner. The Hennards moved a dozen times before George was eighteen. Partly because he moved around so much and partly because he was frightfully strange, George never quite fit into any school cliques and was a mediocre student.

Some who knew him as a boy say he was outgoing and cool, but his personality and behavior literally changed overnight after an argument with his tyrannical father, who chopped George's long dark hair with a scalpel. He was so embarrassed by his haphazard haircut, he ran away, but when he was returned home, an enraged Dr. Hennard shaved him bald.

"He was never the same after that," a classmate said later. "He was completely introverted."

His relationship with his mother Jeanna, who had two children from a prior marriage, was turbulent. A pretty woman who tended to dress far younger than her years, she cooed and called young George her "beautiful boy." But almost from the start, their bond was far more complicated. Their fights were often vile, screaming affairs that sometimes became physical—but at other times, they were warm and loving. Although he deeply craved his mother's approval, years later Hennard would call her a bitch and draw Jeanna's head on the slithering body of a rattlesnake.

By the time he transferred from Maine to a new high school at White Sands Missile Range in New Mexico, Hennard—who now preferred to be called Jo Jo, the way his baby sister Desiree pronounced "George"—yearned to be accepted, especially by the girls who always kept him at arm's length. But he cloistered himself in his room with his rock music and marijuana. The pot mollified the beast inside, submerged him in an artificial serenity.

Jo Jo also bought a drum set, but his rock-star dreams evaporated with every jam session where he plunged into his own alternate musical reality, ignoring the rest of the band, even the music they were playing.

Hennard grew to be a handsome man, just over six feet tall with a trim, 185-pound physique and dark, wavy hair. Women found him attractive at a glance, but up close, his piercing black eyes were unsettling, spooky. Even when women saw past his eyes, he spoke awkwardly and had trouble communicating. Nothing ever went far.

After graduating from high school in 1974, Hennard

joined the Navy. Although he hated taking orders, detested the minorities on his crew, and chafed at the tedium of shipboard work, part of him thrived at sea. He especially loved exotic ports-of-call, where he could marinate his unsound soul in easy drugs and easier women, who never rejected him.

During George's unruly Navy years, his father was given command of the hospital at Fort Hood, near the small town of Killeen, Texas. When Dr. Hennard retired from the Army in 1980, the family settled in the nearby village of Belton, where they bought a sprawling, four-bedroom colonial brick mansion built on four lots.

Life was not so easy for their son. After being disciplined for minor offenses in two captain's masts on the fleet oiler *USS Mississinewa*, Seaman Hennard was transferred to the destroyer tender *USS Dixie*, where he kept his nose clean but earned low performance scores. Three years after he joined the Navy, George's enlistment ended, but the Navy didn't give him a chance to re-up. Although he was honorably discharged, across the bottom of his service record was printed, "Not Recommended for Reenlistment."

At twenty, George Hennard was adrift. The old dark squalls were brewing inside him again. The sea had been taken from him. For the first time in his life, nobody—not his father, his captain, or his absentee conscience—could tell him what to do, and Hennard had never made good decisions on his own.

Four months and a minor pot bust later, Hennard went back to sea. He took a job in the Military Sealift Command, a government-run agency that delivered supplies to the military, and after a few more months, joined the Merchant Marine as a seaman aboard a variety of civilian freighters steaming out of ports on the Gulf of Mexico.

In 1982, Hennard assaulted a black shipmate and his seaman's license was suspended for six months. He went to ground in Texas, near his parents' home in Belton, where he pursued his volatile love-hate relationship with his mother, his loathing of women, and his unrestrained pot habit. A roommate at the time later recalled that Hennard "hated blacks, Hispanics, gays. He said women were snakes. He always had derogatory remarks about women—especially after fights with his mother."

When Hennard returned to sea, he sailed out of San Pedro, California, the main harbor for Los Angeles. He earned up to $5,000 a month, and with few expenses beyond his ninety dollar-a-week flophouse room, he banked most of it. After Jeanna divorced Dr. Hennard in 1983, George generously loaned her large amounts of money. He also paid cash for a brand-new 1987 Ford Ranger pickup with a scintillating metallic blue paint job, and financed a new Cadillac for his mother—a luxury car he obsessively tended for her.

But most of all, he loved being at sea so much that he spent his vacations in distant ports of the Far East and Central America, where he could satisfy his overwhelming cravings for drugs and obedient, non-white prostitutes.

And as it had been all along, it was precisely George Hennard's cravings that sparked his final, fatal decline. In May 1989, marijuana was found in Hennard's shipboard cabin. He was suspended again and sent to a two-week drug treatment program in Houston. Not long after his release, his own father—a medical doctor—would tell a relative that he believed Hennard was schizophrenic, causing a final rift between the father and son, who never spoke again.

On August 23, 1989, George Hennard's seaman license

was revoked for good. The darkest moment in his dark life. He'd never go back to sea.

While he prepared his appeal, he worked odd jobs, from steam-cleaning to construction, never staying anywhere very long. He stayed off and on at the now-vacant Belton mansion, which his mother had won in the divorce but was now trying to sell. He tried to join an Austin blues-rock band, but his heavy-handed, manic style and his old habit of drifting off into a different groove again doomed him. He carped profanely about women he met and always ended up with compliant hookers. His white-hot rage at the world simmered, and his paranoia grew profoundly creepy. When his rootless lifestyle had consumed most of his savings, Hennard moved into his divorced mother's two-bedroom apartment in Henderson, Nevada. Their tangled lives remained sometimes affectionate, sometimes violent.

Once, Jeanna fixed her son up with a single woman who worked with her at Miss Faye's Nail Salon in Henderson. During the short, strange courtship, Hennard took her on a macabre pilgrimage to the site of America's bloodiest mass murder to date: James Huberty's 77-minute lunchtime rampage at a McDonald's restaurant in San Ysidro, California, where twenty-one people died before Huberty was killed by a police sniper in 1984.

The relationship grew tenuous soon after Hennard went on a paranoid rant about being followed by police, and it finally ended in a stormy argument between Hennard and his mother on Christmas morning in 1990. That morning, a raging Hennard stomped out of his mother's house and sat revving his pickup's engine just outside the living room window. His shocked girlfriend feared he was planning to gun the truck through the glass, but instead he roared in reverse out of the driveway and she never saw him again.

Less than two months later, Hennard made a last-ditch appeal to get his seaman's license back. He wrote a two-page letter, claiming he'd suffered more punishment for smoking pot than the drunken captain of the ill-fated Exxon Valdez, who was suspended for only nine months. Playing every angle, Hennard also begged the U.S. Coast Guard (which regulated merchant seamen) to help him kick his drug habit by allowing him to go back to sea—because if he couldn't work as a seaman, "I honestly do not believe I could be rehabilitated from drugs.

"Any person can tell you who has known me that I am not readily adaptable to shore life," Hennard closed his letter. "It stinks! My home is the sea, and it is where I belong."

Despite his mushrooming desperation, Hennard's case wasn't hopeless. The commander of the Coast Guard's Marine Safety Office recommended clemency, but the final decision would be months. After eighteen agonizing months, George Hennard wasn't going to wait much longer.

Also in February and March 1991, an increasingly distraught and deluded Hennard bought two handguns, completely legally. He paid $420 cash for a Glock 17, a lightweight Austrian combat pistol capable of firing eighteen rounds as fast as the shooter can pull the trigger. Reloading with a new seventeen-round clip takes less than two seconds. A month later, he paid $354 cash for a stainless-steel Ruger P89, a workhorse semi-automatic pistol that could fire up to sixteen 9mm bullets before reloading.

On June 5, 1991, Hennard visited the FBI field office in Las Vegas. He told the agent that his civil rights had been violated by a secret cabal of white women who conspired to thwart his love life by spying on him, tapping his phone and spreading lies to prospective employers. Sometimes, he said, they stood in front of his car to prevent him from driving.

But apparently not all women were wicked. For obscure reasons, Hennard eventually developed an obsession with two teenage sisters, Jill Fritz and Jana Jernigan, both pretty and both blond, who lived with their divorced mother Jane Bugg a few doors down from the Belton mansion.

The next day, June 6, he hand-wrote a five-page, disjointed letter to Jill and Jana. In an increasingly delusional script, he cooed sweet hallucinations to the girls as he railed against the "mostly white, treacherous female vipers of [Belton and Killeen] who tried to destroy me and my family."

Suggestively, he wondered if "the three of us can get together someday?"

"I will prevail in the Bitter End!" Hennard promised as he closed. Among the four photographs he folded in the letter was a self-portrait with his drums in the desert. It said: George—Grande, final solo.

Within a week of mailing the letter, Hennard was back in Texas as the caretaker of his mom's Belton mansion. There, he spent his days compulsively washing his truck, meticulously dusting the furniture, making copious notes to himself in journals, calendars, and tape recorders, and videotaping some of his favorite murder programs on TV, including a documentary about Huberty's massacre and the 1988 terrorist bombing of Pan Am Flight 103 over Lockerbie, Scotland.

When potential buyers toured the mansion, Hennard would stalk close behind. He kept some doors locked, including his bedroom. When he spoke to them, as he often did, he would list the home's flaws or chide children who wandered away from their parents. The house was his. Not theirs.

But it wasn't just about the house. When children ran after balls that strayed onto the expansive lawn at Hennard's mansion, he chased them away, shouting curses. Young girls walking past were peppered with suggestive remarks. One friend recalled him passing a girl on the street and yelling out his truck window, "Bitch!"

Darkness descended on George Hennard. He fell even deeper into his obsessions and paranoia. In the wee hours, neighbors could hear his squeaking mountain bike passing up and down the dark streets, aimless and haunting.

Hennard also played, again and again, a song that coruscated along his spine like St. Elmo's fire. It was Steely Dan's "Don't Take Me Alive," a hard-rocking anthem about a killer holed-up against enemies who laugh at him and spread lies, determined to cling to his own dark delusions rather than surrender.

And some days, he followed Jill and Jana to their jobs, or to the market, where he might tease them by popping up unexpectedly from behind a car, or play catch-me-if-you-can in the aisles, then disappear into thin air.

And in the darkest nights, Hennard sometimes crept beneath their bedroom window for hours, smoking cigarettes, tossing butts in a growing pile on the ground, and watching. A few days after the usually docile family Shih-Tzu inexplicably began yelping wildly at shadows in the night, the dog dragged himself into the garage and died. He'd been poisoned.

The girls' mother, Jane, began to have nightmares about George Hennard. In one, she saw him as a night-wraith phantom circling their house until he came crashing through the living room's plate-glass bay window with blazing guns in each hand.

Jane awoke with a start in the electric darkness of her

room. It was only a dream, she thought.

Only a dream.

Before dawn on Wednesday, October 16, 1991, George Hennard rode his creaky bike to the Leon Heights Drive-In for his customary fast-food breakfast. Most mornings, clerk Mary Mead hated to see him walk through the door. He was rude and scary, sometimes pushing other customers out of the way as he demanded service.

Sometimes, he'd spit on other customers' cars as he left.

One recent morning, he glared at her and sounded a warning to no one in particular. "This town had better stop messing with me and my family," he growled, "or something terrible's gonna happen."

But not today. Hennard smiled and said good morning as he picked up his usual items: an orange juice, a sausage-and-biscuit sandwich, some doughnuts, and a newspaper. George's geniality was out of character. It vexed her.

"Three thirty-seven," she told him as she rang up his breakfast.

Hennard grubbed in his pocket, then smiled.

"I don't think I have it," he said. "Can I come back this afternoon and pay you?"

"Sure," she said as he gathered his junk food and pedaled off.

The day before, George Hennard had celebrated his thirty-fifth birthday alone. In his desk calendar, he marked the date with these words: "I am not an animal nor am I a number. I am a human being with feelings and emotions." He spent part of his big day in downtown Belton, bitterly complaining about his water bill, blaming yet another conspiracy against him. By nightfall, he drove to The Nomad, a roadhouse, snack bar, arcade, and gas station rolled into a single rusty corrugated metal building just outside the town limits, for his birthday feast of a burger and fries.

While he ate alone at a small table, he watched the TV over the beer cooler. The evening news was replaying clips of the Senate hearings into Anita Hill's sexual harassment charges against Supreme Court nominee Clarence Thomas. Suddenly, Hennard hurled his half-eaten burger across the room at the screen.

"You dumb bitch!" he screamed. "Now you bastards have opened it for all the women!"

But that was yesterday, when things had been all wrong. This was another day—a day to set things right.

Hennard showered and dressed for the occasion. He buckled his freshly ironed, stonewashed jeans with a Southwestern-tooled leather belt. Over a white T-shirt that said "Ford, the heartbreak of today's Chevy," he buttoned up on a short-sleeved, turquoise shirt whose yokes were embroidered with multi-colored Aztec mazes and desert roses. He chose bright red socks from his drawer, and laced up his brown Rockport Oxfords. He wore no jewelry except his Casio quartz wristwatch with a gold face, and his turquoise- and coral-studded pocketknife.

Before Hennard put his personal destiny in order, he ordered his belongings neatly in the big house. He threw out the birthday card his mother had sent, and put the garbage cans at the curb. Everything was laid out: the shipping boxes for his two guns, his videotapes, his Merchant Marine footlockers, his overseas photos, his journals and notes. And there was a fat folder of legal documents about his Merchant Marine troubles, which had culminated in his dismissal—exactly two years, less one day, before.

Around eleven a.m., he wrote a note to his sister

Desiree, who lived off and on at the mansion, too, and left it on the dining room table:

Desiree,

Enclosed is $100.00 to cover the Water and Electric Bill. Do not pay the phone bill! I am responsible for it. Southwestern Bell violated my Privacy Rights. Therefore they don't get paid. Don't let the people in this rotten town get to you like they done to me. Take care of yourself and be strong.

Love you

Brother Jo Jo

And on his desk calendar, in the square for October 16, 1991, he scribbled: "Life has become a stalemate. There is simply no hope and not a prayer."

So it wasn't hope Hennard carried. Instead, he stuffed a pack of Bristol cigarettes and four pre-loaded clips of 9mm ammunition in his pockets, along with a fistful of loose cartridges. With two semi-auto pistols and more than a hundred rounds, he was ready.

At eleven fifty a.m., George Hennard backed his Ford Ranger out of his Belton driveway and soon turned onto Sparta Road toward U.S. 190. In less than a half hour, he'd be in Killeen to set things right.

More than a hundred-fifty diners jammed the Luby's dining room on this Wednesday lunch hour. A few were Suzanna's friends and patients, whom she greeted warmly as she came in. One of the benefits of living in a safe, small town.

The serving line was long and the Gratias' usual table by the restaurant's front windows was occupied, so they claimed a table on the far side of the dining room, beside a wall of floor-to-ceiling windows. Manager Mark Kopenhaffe joined them for lunch, sitting across from Suzanna, with whom he bantered about politics while keeping one eye on the unrelenting stream of hungry people who continued to spill through the front door. It was going to be a big day. One for the books.

A little after twelve-thirty, the swollen serving line slowed almost to a stop and several tables hadn't been bused, yet customers were still coming. Mark excused himself and went to the cashier's counter to speed things along.

The Gratias had eaten their fill and chatted idly while waiting to thank Mark for lunch. At twelve-thirty nine, mellow Muzak played above the collective hum of friendly diners and the soft, telltale clinking of a dining hall. Hanging pothos ivy plants, potted palms, the gentleness of pastel mauve and emerald green colors, and the sheer draperies softened the feel of a corporate cafeteria, made it innocuous and homey.

So at first, the startling crash was presumed to be a busboy who had dropped a big stack of dishes, usually the worst calamity to befall most bland commercial eateries such as this. But when everyone in the place wheeled around to see not a pile of broken plates, but a monstrous blue pickup truck exploding through the plate-glass windows, bounding into the carpeted dining room, smashing tables, chairs, and people in a slicing shower of glass before coming to a stop twenty feet into the crowded restaurant   well, reason twisted in upon itself.

An accident! Suzanna thought as she rose from her chair to help. Somebody lost control of their truck and crashed into the restaurant. Maybe a heart attack! Maybe they need help!

A few Samaritans rushed toward the truck to aid the helpless driver. One was reaching for the door handle when the driver thrust his left arm out his open driver-side window and fired a gun four times into the serving line, and fired another with his right hand out the rolled-down passenger window. And before the driver's would-be rescuer knew what was happening, he'd been shot three times. He died instantly.

"This is for the women of Belton!" the shooter yelled as he leapt from the truck, a Bristol cigarette still between his lips.

It's a robbery! Suzanna suddenly thought. They're going to come for our purses! She could hear the pop-pop-pop of gunfire, but her view was blocked by the truck, which sat just twenty feet away between her and the shooter. Suddenly, Al turned their table on its side and they crouched behind their meager breastworks, but Suzanna had to watch. She had to know.

After the first burst of pandemonium, an eerie silence fell on the entire tan-colored room as George Hennard began shooting the people closest to his truck, then hunting down others. The killing was easy. People hid under their tables, cowering and trying desperately to make themselves small, invisible, but they couldn't make themselves small enough. Isolated cries erupted with each shot, then died.

"This is for what Bell County did to me and my family!" he shouted cryptically as he fired at anyone who stood or fled. "This is payback! Was it worth it? Was it worth it?"

Suzanna saw his face for the first time less than a minute after he crashed through the window. His face intent but calm, Hennard came around the front of his truck toward her, stopping to aim point-blank at a wounded man's head and pulling the trigger. He shot another one, then another one. Always the head.

What's wrong with this guy? Suzanna's rational brain

was spinning, trying to make sense of the bedlam. Like so many women who'd crossed paths with George Hennard, she was sucked into the paradox of his handsome looks and behavior that humans often don't associate with beauty. *He's not bad looking. What could be so wrong? I'd go out with him*

Then the ghastliness of his purpose dawned on her. This wasn't a robbery. It was a mass murder, like she remembered at that McDonald's in California seven years before. She thought at the time she would have been able to shoot Huberty with her gun if she was there that day. Now here was this freak methodically slaughtering frightened people as calmly as an altar boy lights candles, and he would kill everyone unless he was stopped.

She had a gun! She had a clear shot, a place to steady her aim, and he was less than six paces from her. She'd dropped smaller targets much farther away. She couldn't miss.

Suzanna reached for her purse laying a couple feet away in the warm goo of her uneaten chicken tetrazzini—but she realized to her horror, even before she lifted it from the congealing mess, that her Smith & Wesson wasn't there. It lay safely under her passenger seat a hundred feet away, and a lunatic killer stood between them.

"Wait 'til those fucking women in Belton see this!" Hennard hollered as he shot into a group of school teachers. "I wonder if they'll think it was worth it!"

There was no time for regret. Suzanna began to consider her other alternatives, all bad. She thought of breaking the window and running, but knew it would only call attention in her direction. She thought of stabbing the gunman with a steak knife, throwing a salt shaker at his head, whacking him with her goopy purse while he inserts a fresh clip at the next table.

"The women of Belton and Killeen are vipers," Hennard shouted as he pumped three bullets into the chest of Kitty Davis, a new grandmother who'd come to celebrate a former co-worker's engagement.

Hennard prowled the floor, cool and deliberate, executing crouching patrons point-blank in the head or chest, pausing only to rack new clips into his guns. Witnesses later said he often passed over men to shoot women.

The entire restaurant was eerily silent, except for the pop-pop-pop of Hennard's guns and his profane ranting. Frightened diners hid the best they could, sometimes protected by nothing more than the hands covering their heads, hoping not to attract the killer's attention. Paralyzed by fear. Waiting quietly to die.

"I have to do something," Al Gratia told his daughter as they hid behind their overturned table. "If I don't, he'll kill everyone in the restaurant!"

"Yeah and he'll kill you, too, you son-of-a-bitch!" she screamed as she hung for dear life to her father's golf shirt. She kept waiting for a cop to take the killer down. A seventy-one-year-old man shouldn't be the one. Where were the cops? There were always cops in here!

Al had been a crew chief for a U.S. Army Air Corps bomber squadron in World War II, but he was no John Wayne. He didn't own guns and didn't fish because he couldn't inflict pain on the fish. He taught his children how to shoot with a BB gun, but after Suzanna's brother killed a mourning dove, nobody picked up the gun ever again.

Al just couldn't sit and watch people die, one by one, at the hands of a lone madman. And he knew his wife and daughter would die, too, if he didn't act.

In a split-second, Hennard turned away and Al leapt out of his daughter's grasp. He'd taken only a few steps when Hennard turned back and shot him once in the chest. Al dropped onto his side in the narrow aisle and groaned. He was alive but mortally wounded—and Suzanna knew it.

Instead of coming for Suzanna and her mother, Hennard turned to his right and picked up the systematic slaughter in the front area. Later, she would realize that her father's body probably blocked Hennard's path to them, and with so many targets, it wasn't worth the trouble.

Hennard moved back to the serving area, where many people tried to hide.

"You trying to hide from me, bitch?" he yelled at a woman huddled in a corner just before he killed her.

He emptied his Ruger into several more with a cool dispatch. He'd used up all his pre-loaded Ruger clips so he just set the useless gun on a plate of fried chicken and hush puppies and continued to kill with his Glock.

Returning to the center of the dining room to investigate a mysterious heavy thud, Hennard cornered Olgica Taylor and her daughter Anica McNeil, who clutched her four-year-old daughter Lakeisha.

"Tell people I ain't killing no babies today!" Hennard shouted. "Tell everyone Bell County was bad."

He stepped aside to let Anica and her child flee, and when the young mother wavered, he yelled again, "Get out of here before I kill you both!"

Then he shot Olgica in the face before making another pass through the dining room, killing others as he circled.

In the chaos, people tried desperately to hide. One woman hid in a walk-in freezer and was later treated for hypothermia. A teen-age food preparer curled inside an industrial dishwasher and didn't come out until the next day. Some got away, but most were frozen by their fear, trapped like rats in a box.

Suddenly, another explosion of glass rattled the restaurant, this time from the back. Suzanna feared it might be a second attack by an accomplice, but it wasn't. A six-foot-six, three-hundred-pound mechanic named Tommy Vaughan, a Luby's regular, had thrown his linebacker's body through one of the immense windows at the rear of the dining room and panicked diners now frantically scrambled behind him through the jagged glass.

"Mom, we have to get out of here!" Suzanna yelled, but Suzy had just watched her husband of nearly fifty years gunned down. She was frozen by fear, slumped against the window. Suzanna stood and turned her back to the gunman, fully expecting to feel the thump of a bullet as she lifted her mother to her knees. She knew she'd only feel the impact at first. The burning pain would come later.

"You've got to follow me, mom!" she commanded as she sprinted toward the open window, stumbling over someone and losing a shoe as she fell headlong into a bramble of glass shards outside. Blood streamed from cuts on her hands and arms as she ran with one bloody bare foot across the asphalt toward Mark Kopenhaffe, who'd just emerged from an emergency exit.

"My father's shot in the chest   he's down   " she told her friend as she looked around expecting to see her mother right behind her. "My God, where's my mom? I thought she was right behind me!"

Suzy hadn't followed.

Suzanna tried to go back, but police had finally arrived on the scene and a cop kept her back. Her mother wasn't with the others who'd escaped, and the restaurant's reflective glass hid the carnage inside. The shooting continued as she limped to the relative safety of a nearby apartment complex with other survivors.

There, a tenant loaned Suzanna a phone so she could call her sister in Killeen.

"Get over to Luby's now. There's been shooting. Mom and Dad are in trouble," is all she said.

She also tried to call her brother in Lampasas, too, but only got his answering machine—and in the background of her message were gunshots. Hennard was shooting the straggling diners who had been wounded or hesitated to escape when they had the chance.

When the first cops arrived, they couldn't be sure who the shooter was. One rattled survivor told them it was a black man carrying an assault rifle. And if they saw a man with a gun inside, they couldn't be certain if it was the killer, a vigilante civilian defending himself, or another undercover cop.

But any doubt was erased when State Police Sgt. Bill Cooper, standing outside the shattered window where it all began eleven minutes before, watched a dark-haired white man in a blue, short-sleeved shirt firing at wounded people on the floor and, in a moment, execute an old woman next to the windows on the far side of the dining room. It was Suzy Gratia.

"Police!" one of the cops yelled, but Hennard ignored them.

A Killeen undercover detective, Ken Olson, was one of the first lawmen on the scene. When Hennard showed himself, Olson fired his Browning 9mm from his hip. His bullet passed through the killer's right forearm and lodged below the skin in his chest. Stunned, Hennard retreated to a confined alcove outside the restrooms. He was cornered.

But George Hennard wasn't going down without a fight. He fired several more shots and taunted the cops, who shot back.

"Drop your weapon and come out with your hands up!" Olson's partner Chuck Longwell hollered.

"Fuck you!" Hennard yelled.

"Fuck us? Fuck you!"

"Fuck you! I'm going to kill more people," Hennard taunted again.

A handful of cops slowly closed in on Hennard's hiding place, crawling over dead and wounded bodies as they tightened the noose. This guy wasn't getting out alive unless he surrendered, and that didn't look likely.

After trading a few more shots, Hennard was hit in his left thigh, throwing him against the alcove's back wall. Although he now suffered from at least four flesh wounds, the undaunted Hennard unleashed another fusillade.

"I have hostages!" the killer yelled.

The cops could clearly see he didn't. The profane skirmish continued.

"You don't have any fucking hostages," Olson said.

"I do, too!"

"Show 'em!"

Then Hennard spied a cop crawling belly-down through a breach in the ruined dining room. An easy kill. He raised the Glock for a clear shot and—nothing. His gun jammed. A live shell stuck awkwardly from the breech. In all the chaos, Hennard had mistakenly shoved a Ruger clip in the gun. He dropped to his stomach, hastily cleared the breech and substituted a full Glock magazine he found on the floor, then racked the slide.

It was too late to kill the cop, who now had the drop on

him. But it wasn't too late to make things right.

Hennard rolled onto his back, pressed the Glock against his right temple and pulled the trigger. The bullet exited his left temple and hit the alcove wall, releasing a spew of blood, fragmented brains, and whatever demons haunted him.

The numbers were horrifying. Twenty-two innocent people—eight men and fifteen women—lay dead around Hennard and another died of her wounds later. Seventeen were wounded by gunfire, and sixteen more suffered cuts, broken bones and shock. More than one hundred rounds had been fired in little more than twelve minutes.

One small town wondered why.

And George "Jo Jo" Hennard, who died with his frightening eyes open and lay in a congealing puddle of his own gore, had fired the last shot in the deadliest mass shooting in American history.

The world had missed every sign, every omen.

The killer dropped his jammed gun on a cafeteria tray during the massacre

Al Gratia outlived his killer. When the shooting ended, paramedic Robert Kelley found Al alive but in shock, rolling from side to side, unable to speak or breathe. His pulse was weak, and he was turning deathly blue as he sloped toward unconsciousness. At a glance, Kelley knew Al was mortally wounded, likely drowning in his own blood. Because other lives might be saved in these precious minutes, Kelley made a harsh triage decision. He mentally labeled Al as a likely death.

"Let's get this guy out front, on oxygen," Kelley told an EMT with a stretcher as he continued the grim task of sorting the dead from the living. Muzak still played and a phone rang incessantly somewhere as the Vietnam combat vet circled the wrecked room. Gun smoke and the smell of death hung in the air as he covered each corpse's face with a green linen napkin, a sign to his fellow medics that this one was beyond help.

When he was almost finished, Kelley checked another lifeless man's pulse while a police officer stood over him with an assault rifle.

"Is he dead?" the cop asked.

"Yeah."

"It's a good thing," the cop said, and that's when Kelley knew the dead man was the killer himself.

As Kelley hurried to help with the wounded outside, Suzanna tried in vain to get back into the restaurant to find her mother and father. Refused re-entry at the broken window where she'd escaped, she looked for her lost shoe and limped around to the front of the building, where ambulances were shuttling the wounded to local hospitals, along with a steady stream of med-evac dust-offs from Fort Hood. She pushed her way through a growing throng of reporters, frenzied survivors, overwhelmed first responders, and curious onlookers.

There under the Luby's atrium, out of the direct sun, she found her father's body strapped to a backboard. He had just died. His open eyes were empty and flat, and blood pooled on the asphalt beneath his stretcher. She cursed herself for being slow getting there, for the cuts that slowed her, for worrying about a goddamned shoe. She might have been able to spend her father's dying seconds with him.

"Is there anything I can do?" she asked Kelley, who covered Al's body with a sheet.

"He's gone," the veteran paramedic answered.

Suzanna's sister and brother-in-law, Erika and John Boylan, suddenly burst through the crowded chaos.

"Dad's gone," Suzanna told her as Erika dissolved into tears.

"What about mom?" Erika asked when she regained her composure.

"I've got a bad feeling," Suzanna said, herself close to breaking. "The way the guy was shooting "

The news about Suzy Gratia came later, when survivors were gathered in the neighboring Sheraton Hotel, when friend Mark Kopenhaffe appeared at the door to Suzanna's first-floor room.

"Thank God you're okay!" she said, hugging him.

"Suz, your mom's dead," he told her. "There's nothing I could do."

"How do you know?"

He told her how the cops had watched Hennard kill Suzy, how her death strangely might have saved lives. "Him shooting her   that's how they knew he was the bad guy," Mark said.

Suzy and Al Gratia died as they had lived most of their adult lives. Together.

Suzanna didn't sleep that night. The monstrous movie just kept replaying in her mind, and always with the same bloody ending. In her waking nightmare, her mother Suzy refused to save herself because it would require leaving her beloved Al behind. And every time the horror show looped back on itself, she died with him. No matter how hard she wished, Suzanna couldn't change the ending in her imagination or in reality.

And that night, sleep didn't come easy for Robert Kelley either. In a nightmare, he watched a giant hand materialize from an angry, black cloud, pointing down at him reproachfully. He bolted upright from a cold sweat, frightening his wife. He thought of the old man who reached out to him without words or breath, the man he decided would soon die. How could he have been sure? Was there more he could have done? Numbed by all the death around him, did he give up too quickly on Al Gratia?

Two weeks after the shooting, Al and Suzy Gratia were buried together in the national cemetery in San Antonio to a bone-rattling 21-gun salute that curdled Suzanna Gratia's blood. The acrid stink of gun smoke in the crisp fall air made her sick.

Thankfully, a cadre of psychological counselors had recently been moved to nearby Fort Hood in anticipation of heavy Desert Storm casualties, so survivors and the families of victims received quick attention to their emotional trauma. (The first irony is that Killeen lost twice as many citizens at Luby's than it did in the brief Gulf War; the second irony is that almost exactly nineteen years later, an Army psychological counselor named Nidal Malik Hasan would open fire with two handguns on soldiers just after lunch at Fort Hood, killing thirteen and wounding thirty-two in Killeen's second major mass murder in two decades.)

After George Hennard's ashes began their journey to the sea, Suzanna joined a small group of survivors on a clandestine tour of the killing floor.

Locals had been gossiping that the cafeteria, like the McDonald's in San Ysidro, might be torn down, erased from the community's memory altogether. Instead, Luby's had gutted the restaurant, ripped up the bloody carpeting and scrubbed the bloodstains off the concrete beneath, patched the bullet holes, expelled the stink of burnt gunpowder and death, dumped all the furnishings   exorcised everything but the ghosts that haunted the place.

But on the asphalt outside, in the exact spot under the atrium where her father breathed his last, a dark stain lingered.

It was Al's blood.

The massacre was not yet finished for Suzanna. In her mind, amid the guilt and cold rationale that had failed her when it mattered most, the slaughter of her mother, father, and twenty-one others became part of a bigger battle for survival. If she could replay the day, she would risk everything by carrying her gun into Luby's for a shot at George Hennard, but there were no replays.

She began to think she could change the past by changing the future.

The people of Killeen wore yellow ribbons while troops from nearby Fort Hood were fighting in Iraq, and switched to white ribbons after Hennard's rampage. They left flowers and heartfelt messages outside the empty Luby's shattered windows.

And Texas Gov. Ann Richards spoke passionately about the need to control the sale and possession of automatic weapons, even though Hennard had purchased his guns—

both semi-automatic weapons—completely legally. "Dead lying on the floor of Luby's should be enough evidence we are not taking a rational posture," she said.

For them that was enough, but not for Suzanna.

Suzanna launched a one-woman crusade to allow Texans to carry hidden, loaded handguns if they pass a safety course and get a license. And in 1996, five years after George Hennard's rampage, it became law, although concealed weapons remained illegal in places like churches, stadiums, government offices, courts, airports, and restaurants serving alcohol.

Now married to Greg Hupp, the man she was dating at the time of the Luby's shooting, Suzanna ran for the Texas Legislature and won handily. She continued her crusade for gun rights, testifying passionately in Congress and states where fear of random crime had forced a legislative response.

"I've lived what gun laws do," she told them all. "My parents died because of what gun laws do. I'm the quintessential soccer mom, and I want the right to protect my family. What happened to my parents will never happen again with my kids there."

The media beat a well-worn track to her door. She got air-time with all the major networks and ink in most of the country's magazines and newspapers. She became the first woman ever honored with a life membership in the National Rifle Association.

After serving five terms in the Texas Legislature, Suzanna retired with Greg to raise her two sons on her Central Texas horse farm. She has written an unpublished manuscript about her life, Luby's and gun rights, but mostly she jealously guards her time with her children—one of the post-traumatic effects she must endure.

Suzanna now carries a gun with her almost everywhere, hidden in a purse or holster. She even has a special gun purse for her evening wear. She still eats out at restaurants, preferring places where she's known—and where she knows most everyone. She always sits where she can watch the door, usually near the back. If a strange, lone man saunters in, she pays closer attention. If a dropped glass shatters on the floor, she freezes for a startled moment.

But she's ready.

And she never mentions George Hennard's name, denying him the notoriety that even a single whispered breath grants. He is just "the gunman" or "the killer," her way of reducing him to the pathetic, unfinished, nameless soul that he will always be to her.

Tanya Reid

*The Panhandle Mother
Who Loved Her Baby to Death
By Gregg Olsen*

TANYA REID LOOKED AT THE GRIM FACES OF THE PEOPLE standing near her. Her husband. Her sister. Her parents. Her young daughter. Two detectives.

The moment she'd seen the police drive up, she knew they'd come for her.

"Tanya, you are going to have to come down to the station. We have a warrant for your arrest," one said.

She started to cry. "Could I change my clothes and call my lawyer?" she asked.

He agreed. When she came back downstairs a few minutes later, she turned to seven-year-old Carolyn. "They've taken Michael away from us, and now they're taking me away!" she cried out.

Tanya was doing what she always did, putting herself before what was best for her children, gulping the attention.

The detective tried to soothe the child, but Tanya had done a good job of agitating Carolyn. Her brother, three-year-old Michael, had been removed from the family and was in foster care. Now her mother was about to be led away by police.

At the Urbandale, Iowa police station Tanya Thaxton Reid was formally charged with endangering Michael's life.

Soon, authorities in Texas would be investigating the death of another of her children, her baby daughter, Morgan.

She, and many who knew her, were stunned by the accusations.

Tanya was a devoted wife and mother. She rocked her children to sleep every night. She had dinner on the table for her husband when he came home from work and she kept a clean house. She was a LVN, a licensed vocational nurse, helping patients – including babies – with day-to-day challenges they faced when hospitalized. She had literally saved the lives of her own children by breathing oxygen into their tiny mouths. She kept a vigil at their bedside during dozens of hospitalizations for a terrible genetic disease she said they had.

Tanya? Responsible for her baby daughter's death and the near-death of her son? It was impossible. She loved her children to death.

THE URBANDALE POLICE HAD NEVER HEARD OF MUNCHAUSEN SYNDROME by Proxy (often shortened to MSP or MSBP). Not many people had when the first of Tanya Reid's children died in 1984, or even in 1988 when doctors who treated Michael and state child protection investigators finally began to put the pieces together.

"Munchausen syndrome" was coined by a doctor in 1951 writing in the British medical journal Lancet (the name refers to the eighteenth-century adventurer Baron Von Munchausen, who told tall tales about his exploits in war). The doctor used the term to describe patients who faked illnesses to receive unnecessary medical care and the attention and sympathy that accompanies it. It wasn't until 1977 that another doctor wrote in Lancet about two mothers who had inflicted illnesses on their children and received the same attention "by proxy."

Tanya Thaxton was the fourth and last of the daughters born to John and Wanda Thaxton in their middle-class neighborhood in Dumas, a town in the Texas Panhandle. Tanya once described herself this way: "I was raised as a Baptist. I was in the youth choir, and I sang in the church there. I played in the high school band. I played clarinet. Went to all the football games and basketball games. Just a normal growing up."

After graduating from high school in 1976, Tanya began the vocational nursing program at Dumas Memorial Hospital, where as part of her duties she helped care for the babies in the nursery. At about the same time she met her family's new next door neighbor, Jim Reid. He was seven years older than Tanya and was working for Swift Independent Packing Company, a meat-packing plant. He was the quiet one and Tanya was the more out-going partner. They married in 1977.

The Reid's daughter, Carolyn, born in 1981, didn't seem to have any health problems. But from the day her sister was born in May, 1983, little Morgan Renee seemed to struggle for her life.

Just days after her birth Tanya rushed Morgan to the hospital saying she had a strange rash and colic. Doctors said she was healthy, but suggested Tanya stop breastfeeding and try a supplement. She did and the rash disappeared. Later, Tanya resumed nursing.

Lots of babies are allergic to breast milk or colicky, but Tanya was dramatic about even the simplest sniffle. Neighbors said that if they heard sirens, they knew an ambulance was on its way to the Reid's house.

Tanya loved the attention. Nurses admired the way she wouldn't leave Morgan's side. Other mothers would share the usual worries about their children but no one could top Tanya's stories. She thrived on the attention and sympathy.

Tanya learned quickly that Jim's career at Swift made her something akin to a military wife. They moved, and then moved again for his work, back and forth between Texas, Illinois and Iowa. The constant buying and selling of houses, with temporary stays in motels or apartments, were hard on the marriage. So were the children's illnesses.

It meant that Tanya didn't only fool her husband, parents and friends about her children's health. She fooled doctors in three states.

In August, 1983, when Morgan was just three months old, she stopped breathing for the first time. Tanya saved her by giving her mouth to mouth resuscitation. Tanya told her parents that Morgan had experienced a seizure and stopped breathing. She said doctors told her it was a SIDS (Sudden Infant Death Syndrome) near-miss. At the time, SIDS was a catchall designation assigned to cases in which otherwise healthy infants mysteriously stopped breathing, usually during sleep, and died.

In February, 1984 when the girl was just nine months old, there was another seizure. Tanya didn't save her this time. Morgan was hospitalized and when doctors said she was brain dead, life support was removed. For a few hours she struggled to live, then died in her mother's arms.

Morgan was buried wearing a yellow pinafore and white tights, with a white bonnet on her head to try and conceal incisions made during the autopsy. The conclusion was that Morgan most likely died of SIDS. It would take years, but physicians and pathologists would eventually have a keener understanding of just how often child abuse and infanticide – from SHS (Shaken Baby syndrome) and MSBP – was responsible for the death of children.

Tanya and Jim stopped attending church. She told friends that their minister didn't seem sympathetic and didn't understand her anger at God.

"There's all these people who commit crimes—rapists, murderers—or even those dying of cancer. Why did God have to take an innocent child and not one of them? Why did he have to do that?" she cried.

A FEW MONTHS AFTER MORGAN'S death, Jim was transferred back to Chicago and the family moved again. Tanya became pregnant. She fainted several times and each time she did she received some much-needed attention from the aloof Jim. On May 2, 1985, she gave birth to a ten-pound boy, Brandon Michael, who they called Michael. He was a "happy, happy baby," Tonya said. "He slept through the night, never bothering us a bit."

The day after his birth, Tanya had her tubes tied. It was too risky to have more children, she told friends, because "there's a problem with our genes."

The happiness was short-lived. When Michael was just 26 days old, Tanya called the paramedics: She had found him unconscious and was performing mouth-to-mouth resuscitation to keep him alive.

By the time Michael was two, the family had left Illinois and moved back to Texas, and then on to Des Moines, Iowa for Jim's job. Tanya told Michael's doctors during his frequent medical appointments that Morgan had died of SIDS and that Michael had frequent bouts of apnea – seizures when he would stop breathing, turn blue and seem glassy-eyed. She would resuscitate him and hurry to the hospital.

Just two days after their move to Iowa, Tanya rushed Michael to the emergency room. She said that he had had a seizure and resuscitated him. Nurses noticed the unusual relationship between mother and son. Some felt the boy was lucky to have such a concerned mother who never left his side. But notes about Tanya's mothering began to show up in hospital charts. One nurse wrote: *"Mom and child interaction somewhat inappropriate, i.e. seem antagonistic toward each other "*

Hospital staff noticed that while waiting to be admitted, Tanya seemed excited, grinning as she greeted the doctors and nurses she knew with a big smile, almost "showing off." It was like a social event to Tanya. They also watched at how disturbed Michael seemed when Tanya returned from grabbing some food in the cafeteria. One time, from his hospital crib, he cried out, "Mom - go!"

Hospital staff referred her to a counselor. Tanya seemed agitated when discussing her son and his health concerns but when the counselor suggested the entire family could benefit from therapy, Tanya agreed it might be a good idea. The young mother also talked about Morgan's death, prompting the counselor to write in her report: *"I believe this issue (SIDS death) is unresolved for her."*

Tanya took Michael to the doctor dozens of times. They knew she was an unusually attentive mother, even paranoid, but decided it was because she had lost a baby girl.

In my book about Tanya Reid, *Cruel Deception – A Mother's Deadly Game, A Prosecutor's Crusade for Justice,* I described the moment when doctors finally wondered if they were seeing what for most of them was their first case of MSBP:

Brandon Michael Reid was a beautiful little boy with blondish hair that just brushed over the tops of his ears. His eyes were bright and blue, the color of his father's. He was the calendar boy for the American Heartland. Under ordinary circumstances he would be the apple of anyone's eyes. But at 12:14 p.m. on February 7, 1988, he was not a little kid playing in a grassy field, or rolling on the floor with a puppy. He was sweaty and terrified. His hair was matted in whorls onto his forehead. Despite the fact that it was lunchtime, he hadn't even been dressed for the day.

Instead, he had been fighting for his life. Fighting for air. This one would be recalled as the episode that was very different—in its beginning and its outcome. Jim Reid was not at the office; he was at home enjoying the lull of a Sunday afternoon. He was not in the yard. Not at the neighbors. Not in the garage. Jim Reid was in the house. His son and wife were upstairs in the master bedroom playing. He could hear Tanya and Michael laughing and giggling. It was a good sound. The sound of a happy family. After all they had been through, good times were cherished, savored. Then the noise stopped. It was quiet upstairs, as though the volume control of a TV had been turned off. It was an abrupt, slamming silence. A moment later, Jim lurched in the direction of Tanya's screams.

"Jim, come quick! It's Michael! He had another spell!"

Jim climbed the stairs and rushed into the bedroom. Michael, sweaty and limp, was on the bed. Tanya hovered over their son doing mouth-to-mouth.

"Have you called paramedics?"

Between breaths, Tanya said she had.

Jim checked his son's heart rate and studied the boy's blue, still face for any sign that he'd be all right. In a minute, even before the paramedics came, Michael was breathing on his own. And by all accounts, the little boy was angry. Michael wore a two-piece pajama set as he was carted kicking and wailing across the glint of linoleum of the emergency room at Blank Children's Hospital that Sunday afternoon. The child was not a stranger to the staff working that shift. Dr. Robert Colman and Dr. Anne Zoucha had seen the little boy before. They also knew his mother. They knew the routine. But this time it would be different. ER nurse Callie Sandquist watched as they put the Reid boy into Trauma 1, one of a pocket of five examination rooms directly across from the nurses' station. The little boy was screaming. Not crying, but absolutely howling. He was not saying any words, just making noise.

Callie would later try to describe the boy's state. "He was inconsolable. . . . You can't make him stop, it doesn't matter what you do. It's almost like being hysterical." The nurse scrutinized his mother. Tanya Reid was a short, pleasant woman with neatly done dark hair and dressed in a simple pullover top and jeans. She was very calm as she stood talking to Drs. Colman and Zoucha and described what had happened at home. The scene seemed odd to Callie, who had worked at the hospital for seventeen years and thought she had seen it all. Something was wrong with the picture.

"If it was my kid doing that I wouldn't be able to stand that for very long. But she was over in the corner talking to the doctor, and she just kept going on and on with this long detailed history using all the appropriate phrases, technical terms, long medical names—I mean, I wouldn't have been able to have remembered them," she would later say. Tanya seemed oblivious to Michael's caterwauling. Never once did she step over to soothe her son. "It didn't seem to bother her. She was just over there chatting with the doctors."

Later, none of the nurses could recall any details about the little boy's father. Jim Reid was there, nurses said, but he stayed out of the fray and let his wife handle everything.

The atmosphere in the ER took a decided turn when Dr. Zoucha, the pediatrician running the show that night, barreled out of Trauma 1 and slammed the little patient's charts against a countertop. An attractive woman and usually a calming influence, Dr. Zoucha was not given to such outbursts of emotion.

She was a healer, not an antagonizer. But she was furious. Her words shocked.

"She's smothering that kid!"

Pediatric resident Colman, also taken back by his colleague's anger, nodded in agreement. "Yes," he said, recalling his earlier suspicions, "this has been going on way too long."

A call was made to the Iowa Department of Human Services for a child protective investigator. The little boy screaming in the ER was a victim of a rare form of child abuse. The alleged abuser was his mother. Both Dr. Colman and Dr. Zoucha believed Michael suffered from Munchausen Syndrome by Proxy. They suspected his mother was smothering him because of her own need for attention, specifically from medical staff.

Nurse Sandquist was horrified and intrigued. She had never seen an MSBP case before. The veteran nurse drew closer to the patient and his mother as she searched for clues that could reveal what had happened that afternoon. Reporting an allegation of child abuse was serious. Details were a necessity. Written backup would be critical.

In addition to his incessant screams, something else about the supposed seizure patient appeared noteworthy. Brandon Michael Reid had four scratches on his cheek—parallel abrasions that looked as if they could have been made by fingernails. Two were deep enough to bead minute rows of blood. Since the scratches were small, it suggested to Callie they had been made by the child. His lower left eyelid was also flushed with the subtle purple of a fresh bruise.

Tanya Reid, seemingly oblivious to the turmoil brewing around her, accosted the nurse and held out her right index finger. It, too, was scratched. At the nail bed it bled slightly. "I hurt my finger," she said. "Can I get a bandage?"

The little boy had been admitted to the hospital by the time a child protective investigator arrived, about two-thirty that afternoon. Investigator Mark Gillespie had been notified by pager and made the trip to the hospital as soon as he could. Gillespie first met with Dr. Zoucha, who filled him in on some of the boy's medical history. She told him Michael had been admitted to Blank several times, most recently about three weeks prior.

Dr. Zoucha pointed out the scratches on the boy and his mother. She told the investigator the scratches might be a result of Michael's attempt to stop his mother from suffocating him. While they were admitting the child for observation of any seizures, it was primarily a means of protecting the boy. Foster care, she said, was the long-term answer. "I have no doubt," she said, "that the mother is trying to suffocate the child and the child is in danger."

Dr. Robert Colman, the pediatrics resident who was among the first to suggest Michael Reid was the victim of Munchausen Syndrome by Proxy, was every mother's dream of a pediatrician. Sympathetic blue eyes, ready smile, and gentle manner conveyed a genuine love for children. Investigator Gillespie met with the young doctor for a briefing before interviewing Jim and Tanya Reid, who still had no idea about the allegations. Dr. Colman advised the investigator of some of the background of the Reids, including how they had moved a number of times and

Michael had been to numerous hospitals for testing, most recently the Mayo Clinic.

"Mayo reportedly declined to do any testing," he said, "indicating there was nothing wrong with the child."

Mark Gillespie sat down to take it all in, filling his notebook with information on a condition about which he had known little. Then it was time to see the Reids. It was 4:00 p.m. and Michael had calmed down in his room on the third floor. He was outfitted in flimsy hospital pajamas colored with some obscure cartoon character, and blue fleecy slippers were by his feet. Soon he would sleep.

Jim Reid stood alone, stunned and mute when the abuse investigator identified himself and stated the purpose of his visit. Michael's father's face exhibited the affect that Mark Gillespie had seen all too often, a combination of shock and indignation.

There must be some mistake.

Jim immediately picked up the phone to call Tanya, who, he explained, had gone home with their daughter Carolyn to change clothes. His voice was hushed, his words sparse. "Tanya, there's a man here to talk to us. They are accusing us of smothering Michael."

Tanya started to shake as she told her husband that she'd be right over. She couldn't believe what she was hearing. "I went totally to pieces," she said later. "I was mad and scared." Tanya left Carolyn at Staci's and made her way to Michael's hospital room to take a seat next to Jim as they faced the investigator. She could explain everything. The interview would last forty-five minutes.

"We didn't know what to think," Tanya said later of the allegations and the interview. "We didn't have anything to hide. We willingly talked to Mark. I told him I was mad, and he said he understood. This was an ordeal for us." Tanya called her sister Rodena to talk about the allegations and about getting an attorney. Tanya was upset, but she was sure she'd be vindicated. This was all a mistake, after all. It would blow over. In case it didn't, the Thaxton family called on Esther Hayward, a Dallas attorney and friend of Rodena and her husband's, to make inquiries about finding a good lawyer in Des Moines. Esther reported back that it was Bill Kutmus's name that came up most often. Tanya also tried to seek help from a member of an association she had seen on the "700 Club" television program. The group, Victims of Child Abuse Laws (VOCAL), had formed to clear the sullied names of parents falsely accused of child abuse. Tanya related how she was uncomfortable with the Iowa doctors and was convinced they were on some kind of child abuse witch-hunt. But because of the early stage of the investigation, the VOCAL member was unable to help. The Reids were on their own.

Jim Reid stood firm with his wife in her denial that she could have done anything to hurt their son or daughter. He proclaimed great certainty that in the end Tanya would be vindicated. He held no doubts that she was an attentive mother. He said later, "She's always real careful about how the kids look and how they dress and how they act and tries to teach them right from wrong and takes time to participate in their activities."

OTHER HOSPITALS SET UP HIDDEN VIDEO CAMERAS to see if a parent interfered with their child's treatment. Cameras had caught mothers – and more rarely, dads – putting a pillow over a child's face, or contaminating urine or vomit samples with their own blood. One mom repeatedly rubbed a noxious oven cleaner all over her child's back to produce a ghastly rash.

But the Iowa hospitals treating Michael were worried about the invasion of privacy and the headlines that might result if the public found out they were surreptitiously spying on parents.

Investigators and physicians agreed that the only fail-safe way to establish a MSBP diagnosis with Michael was to separate mother and son. If his "spells" stopped, the diagnosis could be made. But how could they get the boy away from his mother?

Investigators with the Polk County district attorney's office began piecing together Tanya's history. The more they learned about her, the more they saw how she met the criteria of a MSBP parent:

- Tanya worked in health care.
- She was alone with Morgan and Michael whenever they had a seizure or "spell".
- The "spells" only happened on certain days and certain times of day.
- Tanya lied and told investigators that a physician had witnessed one – he hadn't.
- Tanya *wanted* her child to be at the hospital, and she was never far from their side.
- She seemed "excited" by the attention.
- Her husband was often absent from the home and also never witnessed a "spell".

Were there any clues in Tanya's own background? Her mother, Wanda, had health problems when Tanya was young. Tanya liked the attention and felt loved when her mother was sick or when she was sick. She remembered a time when her mother was hospitalized. An aunt took Tanya, just a preschooler, to the hospital to have a small cyst removed from under her left arm. She was terrified of the rubber ether mask pressed against her face, but was left with a warm memory from the experience. "They put me in mother's room," Tanya remembered later, "and mother picked me up and moved me in bed with her. She held me next to her for hours and hours."

Bad luck and freak accidents plagued Tanya. She stubbed her toe and it became badly infected. While playing hide-and-seek one summer afternoon, Tanya crashed her left arm through a plate glass window, severing an artery. Her mother wondered if her daughter was born unlucky. The girl had a knack for caring for wounded animals. One of her sisters said Tanya "always wanted the miracle of saving a life," and as a child tried to save wounded birds.

TO DETERIMINE IF TANYA REID WAS HARMING HER SON MICHAEL, investigators had to look closely at Morgan Renee's death, several years before. Maybe what they learned would help them protect Michael.

Although Polk County assistant county attorney Melodee Hanes had read that it was nearly impossible to prove that a mother suffered from MSBP syndrome, she set her sights on Tanya. She spent months hunting down nearly every doctor who had seen Tanya's children over the years.

She received a copy of Morgan Renee Reid's autopsy report from Northwest Texas Hospital in Amarillo, a report that concluded there was "no evidence of child abuse." But pathologists in Iowa discovered that an x-ray taken during the autopsy revealed that Morgan did *not* die of SIDS but showed brain damage consistent with being shaken violently.

Hanes tracked down the pathologist who had conducted Morgan's autopsy. He had left Texas and was practicing in Arkansas. He explained that he wrote that there was no evidence of abuse because he had found no bruises or fractures. He admitted he had never heard of Shaken Baby Syndrome.

A hospital trauma team concluded that Michael Reid was in imminent danger and that it was a case of MSBP. He should be removed from the home. They decided Carolyn Reid was safe because she was old enough to speak up if she was harmed.

That's when two detectives and a juvenile court officer drove to an Urbandale day care center to take Michael into custody. They felt as if they were just in time.

As soon as Michael was removed from Tanya's care, his health was fine. Tanya said Michael must have outgrown the spells.

IN FEBRUARY, 1989 TANYA THAXTON REID WAS CONVICTED OF felony abuse of Michael. She was sentenced to ten years in the women's prison in Mitchellville, Iowa. She never appealed, but maintained her innocence. Jim and Tanya divorced, in part so he would get custody of Carolyn and Michael, and he remarried.

On December 13, 1993 a Texas jury found Tanya guilty of first degree murder for the death of Morgan Renee. She was sentenced to 62 years in prison. Two years later, an appellate court overturned her conviction. She returned to her hometown of Dumas, Texas and worked at a McDonalds. In 1996, Tanya Thaxton Reid, now thirty-eight years old, was re-tried, turned down a plea deal, and was sentenced to serve 40 years in a women's prison in Gatesville, Texas.

She was paroled in 2008. She had hoped to move to California and start a new life, but she lives where she spent her childhood and much of her life as a mother, in Texas.

Her ex-husband and daughter have stood by her.

Tanya's son, Michael, is one of the few family members with no contact with Tanya. He reportedly suffered permanent hearing loss which he believes was caused by his mother's abuse.

The question of how far back Tanya's compulsion to harm her children, and bask in the attention, went was answered in part during her first trial when prosecutors found what they considered "the smoking gun." It was a story that Tanya, her parents and her siblings neglected to share with doctors or the police.

In 1974, when Tanya Thaxton was seventeen years old, she was babysitting four-month-old Scotty Simmons while his parents attended a church meeting. It wasn't her first time babysitting Scotty.

During the evening, Scotty quit breathing. It was before the 9-1-1 system existed, so Tanya called an operator, who called the police, who sent an ambulance.

Scott was revived but was never the same. Although he suffered brain damage from lack of oxygen and has cerebral palsy, Scotty excelled in school and graduated with honors.

Both Tanya and a police officer were honored for helping Scotty. Tanya was named the recipient of the Ladies' Chamber of Commerce Good Neighbor Award. A presentation was held at a restaurant.

The newspaper ran two articles. The headline of the first was "Police officer saves life of city infant." The second was: "Quick reaction to emergency: Tanya Thaxton, babysitter, receives good neighbor award."

Tanya said the Scott Simmons incident was a turning point in her life, but not for the reason people think. "It just amazes me that people are now saying that the Good Neighbor Award made me want to kill my own children," she said. "It helped persuade me to get into medical care. At the time, I couldn't help that baby. I didn't know how to do CPR. I just sat there, helpless, until the police came. And from then on, I wanted to be prepared."

She couldn't believe that the prosecutor would dredge up the story. "They said I did this because I wanted to get attention; then what caused me to do it in the first place? I didn't know I was going to get the Good Neighbor Award. We only kept it for a month. They engrave your name in one of the little squares, you kept it a month, and you had to give it back. It's not like I got a big trophy I keep in my house."

MUNCHAUSEN SYNDROME BY PROXY IS NOW called Factitious Disorder Imposed on Another. In the thirty years since nine-month-old Morgan Renee Reid died, physicians have learned more about MSBP. It most often occurs in mothers, although it can occur in fathers, who intentionally harm their children in order to receive attention. It can also show up in people who take care of the elderly, the disabled, and pets.

The diagnosis is not given to the victim, but rather to the perpetrator.

In 2007, Scott Simmons, the infant Tanya Thaxton Reid babysat when she was seventeen years old, posted a letter about his life on the Internet.

"My name is Scott Simmons, and I have cerebral palsy. Cerebral palsy is a broad term that covers anybody who has lost brain cells due to a lack of oxygen. Most people get CP during childbirth, but my story is a bit different.

For the first four months of my life I was a healthy baby. I was born July 1974 in Amarillo Texas, and my parents lived in a small town about an hour north called Dumas. One night in

October while my parents were at a church function, I mysteriously quit breathing while a highly recommended babysitter named Tanya Thaxton was watching me .

The next several years were the hardest for me and my parents. Doctors performed numerous tests on me to figure out what caused me to quit breathing, but they couldn't find any answers. I had several mild and severe seizures, and I spent many hours in physical therapy. And thru all this, I still didn't realize that anything was different about me. As far as I knew, I was as normal as any of my friends were. In fact, I thought my physical therapy was playtime!! When I was 6, I even got involved in little league sports. I played little league T-ball. (Catcher was my favorite position because I got to put the ball back on the tee when kids missed it and knocked it off.) I also played soccer and ran track. I was very competitive, and I hated to lose.

Around that time I began to notice that there was something a little different about me. Even though I practiced as much as possible, I wasn't improving. I couldn't understand why. I also couldn't understand why I had so much trouble staying on a bike when all my friends were learning to ride without training wheels. Many of the kids in elementary school poked fun at my posture and the way I held my hands. It was so frustrating. Why couldn't I get it right?...

My parents thought that it was time to tell me what I had and what had happened to me when I was a baby. After they told me everything I remember feeling a sense of relief that I finally knew why I struggled so much, but I also remember wishing that it had never happened.

My parents made sure that every other part of my life was as normal as possible. They had me focus on things that I could do instead of things I couldn't do. I always loved music, and I loved to sing. When I was eight they took me out of sports and I started piano lessons and I sang in a children's church choir. My piano teacher told me that I had l almost perfect pitch!!

Around that same time I accepted Jesus as my savior and was baptized. I grew up in the church, and had always heard about God's unconditional love. I felt like I was old enough to accept it and to understand it. What I didn't understand at the time was that God had a plan for me

In 1989, our family got a call from the assistant DA in Amarillo who was an old friend of my parents from Dumas. He said that a lady named Tanya Reid was on trial in Des Moines, Iowa for child endangerment, and the DA up there wanted to talk to them. When asked why, he said that she was the same girl who was with me the night I quit breathing. Apparently the same thing happened to her son – several times

The mystery was finally solved. We are pretty sure that Tanya caused my apnea somehow. After we found out about the first trial my parents sat me down to talk to me about it. I told them that I had forgiven her. I don't know if it was my childhood innocence or the Holy Spirit or both working in my heart. But I felt no bitterness towards her. I remember just feeling sorry for her. They said she had Munchausen's Syndrome by proxy. In other words she hurt her children to get attention. She had a disorder just like me, but her disorder was mental, and mine is physical. To this day I have no anger in my heart towards her.

After I tell people this story, their first reaction is always this. "How come you are not angry??" To that I always tell them that if I had any bitterness towards Tanya, it would only hurt me. There is no point. There is nothing I can do about it. I can only look ahead and make the best out of what I can do NOW."

AT THE CONCLUSION OF HER FIRST MURDER TRIAL, I met with Tanya Reid while conducting research for my book, *Cruel Deception*.

Later I wrote:

In many ways I am torn by Tanya Thaxton Reid, a woman who needs help, but cannot allow herself to seek it. As she sat shaking in the Deaf Smith County Jail after the murder verdict came in, I could see tears that were undeniably real. I told her I didn't think she meant to kill Morgan, no matter what actually transpired that frigid, snowy day in Hereford.

"Thank you, thank you I appreciate that," she answered, brightening a bit. I felt such sorrow for her. I wanted to reach under the pass through screen and pat her hand and tell her how sorry I was. So sorry for her family and children, especially her children. Was this the role others had assumed? Is this what she wanted? I'll never know.

EVIL
AT THE
FRONT DOOR

Ron Franscell
and
Rebecca Morris

Copyright 2014 by Gregg Olsen, Rebecca Morris and Ron Franscell
All Rights Reserved
Book Cover Design by BEAUTeBOOK
Cover original photography: Infrogmation of New Orleans @ wikimedia
Map by Brad Arnesen
No part of this publication may be reproduced, stored in a retrieval system, or transmitted, in any form or by any means, electronic, mechanical, photocopying, recording, or otherwise, without the written permission of the authors.
Evil at the Front Door is excerpted from the book Delivered From Evil (Fair Winds Press) © 2011 Ron Franscell
Published by Notorious USA

From the Notorious USA Team

WELCOME TO THE LATEST INSTALLMENT in the *New York Times* bestselling series of stories about America's most notorious criminals.

That's right. No matter where you live, you're in the middle of Notorious USA.

Here, you'll find some of the South's most despicable murderers a woman kills for love; a phantom gunman terrorizes New Orleans; a man is left to die in an alligator-infested bayou.

We're shocked by most crimes, sickened over others, and laugh at a very few. Most are committed in the name of love and greed, but the bottom line is they're stupid people doing stupid things.

We've written about some of these cases before. As time passes we learn more about the criminal and about what makes them tick, about their crimes, and about their victims.

Here's our expert take on several notorious criminals and, incidentally, how they're spending their time these days.

Most are locked up, doing time, and paying their debt to society. To do otherwise would be a crime.

Don't miss *Bodies of Evidence*, Notorious USA's first boxed set and *New York Times* bestselling collection about the criminals from our neck of the woods (the Pacific Northwest). Like all of our collection, *Bodies of Evidence* is available as an eBook on most formats, as well as in paperback and as an audio book.

Your crime scribes,

Gregg Olsen
Ron Franscell
Rebecca Morris

Notorious Louisiana

EXECUTED FOR LOVE

How murder got in the way of a true romance

Some stories are about love, and some are about pain. But painful love stories like the star-crossed romance between Annie Beatrice McQuiston and Claude "Cowboy" Henry started long before they met in a whorehouse on a humid night in Depression-era Texas.

JOE CALLOWAY DIED NAKED IN A LOUISIANA RICE FIELD, trembling with terror and cold, praying to God and begging for his life in the dark.

At that moment, the Houston tire salesman must have regretted stopping near the East Texas border town of Orange to give a lift to the pretty woman and her male companion hitchhiking on this freezing Valentine's night. It was 1940, the Depression was lingering, and people were still in bad shape. Worse, a cold front had moved in, and he probably felt sorry for this couple out on the frigid roadside.

But whatever good deeds he'd done meant nothing. The ride would be short.

Somewhere near Lake Charles, Louisiana, the woman pulled a .32-caliber pistol and forced Calloway to pull over. She and her accomplice stole his wallet containing $15 and forced him into the trunk of his Ford V-8 coupe.

The hitchhikers drove into the deserted rice fields south

of Lake Charles, away from the highway and lights. They forced Calloway to strip naked and marched him at gunpoint to a hidden place behind a stack of rice stalks in a dark field.

Calloway pleaded tearfully with his abductors, but the gun-wielding woman forced him to kneel in the rice stubble and say his prayers. When he finished, she shot him in the forehead, just over his right eye.

Later, Toni Jo Henry would decide her murder of a kindly husband and father wasn't all that cold-blooded. She had, after all, let him finish his prayers.

But the senseless murder of Joe Calloway was just part of Toni Jo's plan to bust her husband, a cop-killer and ex-boxer named Claude "Cowboy" Henry, out of a Texas prison where he was serving 50 years for murder. She and her cohort, a truck-driving Army deserter named Arkie Burks, had already robbed a gun store. Now they needed a car to rob a bank in Camden, Arkansas, where they'd get enough money to bribe Texas prison officials to shorten Cowboy's sentence.

Toni Jo and Burks drove all night to Camden, where they booked a fleabag room. While Toni Jo slept, the spooked Burks fled with Calloway's car and the escape plan fell apart. Toni Jo used the rest of Calloway's $15 to slink back to her hometown of Shreveport, Louisiana, to hunker down.

Toni Jo told her disbelieving family that she'd witnessed a killing and surrendered her gun—minus one bullet. When she was arrested a few days later, Toni Jo took police to Calloway's body. She told them Arkie Burks had pulled the trigger, but when Burks was busted a couple days later, he pointed the finger at Toni Jo.

The cops in Lake Charles didn't care. They would both face the death penalty.

TONI JO HENRY STARTED LIFE AS ANNIE BEATRICE MCQUISTON, the third of five children born to a Shreveport railroader. She grew up poor in the row houses near the tracks. Her mother died of tuberculosis when Annie was six, and when her abusive father remarried, she grew increasingly unhappy at home before moving in with an aunt.

She quit grade school for a job at the Shreveport Macaroni Factory, but was fired when her bosses learned her mother had died of consumption. At only thirteen, with no way to support herself, the petite, dark-haired, and pretty Annie turned to prostitution, a hard life that introduced her to violence, drugs, smoking, and liquor. By sixteen, still drifting among the brothels of Louisiana and Texas, she was a full-fledged cocaine addict and alcoholic.

By 1939, she'd changed her name to Toni Jo. She was turning tricks in a Beaumont, Texas, whorehouse when she met a down-and-out former heavyweight boxer named Claude "Cowboy" Henry, and they immediately fell in love.

Cowboy had been married before, but his wife divorced him and took their son. He'd fought nineteen local prizefights, winning more than he lost and knocking out six of his opponents, who were mostly palookas trying to earn a little cash in the early years of the Depression. These days, though, he only worked as a bouncer and other odd jobs.

Cowboy was uncomfortable with Toni Jo's addictions, maybe even more than her profession, and he determined to help her kick her many habits. Not long after they met, Cowboy locked Toni Jo in a hotel room for a down-and-dirty detoxification. Toni Jo confronted her demons while Cowboy nursed her tenderly. When they emerged, Toni Jo was clean.

On November 25, 1939, they married and embarked on

a quick honeymoon to California. But wedded bliss quickly turned to trouble: In Los Angeles, Cowboy got a telegram saying he'd been indicted in the 1937 shooting death of a San Antonio store cop.

Toni Jo wanted to run, but Cowboy was confident he'd beat the rap. He swore it had been a matter of self-defense. His new wife had her doubts, but she returned to Texas with him to face the charge.

It didn't go well. Within a few weeks, Cowboy was quickly convicted of murder and sent to the state prison in Huntsville for 50 years.

Widowed by a judge, Toni Jo was furious. At Cowboy's sentencing she vowed she'd do everything in her power to get him out of jail—a promise that set a greater tragedy in motion. Less than a month later, Joe Calloway would cross paths with Toni Jo Henry, who had a plan to spring her beloved Cowboy from prison.

And Calloway became collateral damage in her plot.

THE ARREST OF A SULTRY SOUTHERN BEAUTY IN A BIZARRE, RANDOM MURDER that involved love, drugs, and sex made national headlines, even in pre-World War II America.

Toni Jo's first trial opened in Lake Charles on March 27, 1940. It was half lynch-mob, half circus, with angry mobs screaming for her swift death. "Hang her!" somebody yelled in the courtroom. "Hang the bitch!" Defense lawyers even argued that their arguments were occasionally drowned out by the din of onlookers and news photographers.

The defense tried to blame Burks for the murder, but the jury didn't believe them. They deliberated only seven hours before finding Toni Jo guilty and sentencing her to die by hanging. (Burks didn't evade justice, though. He was also convicted a few months later, and also sentenced to death.)

Toni Jo appealed on the grounds that the lynch-mob atmosphere had prejudiced her case, and she was retried in February 1941. This time, Burks testified against her and, again, the jury took only an hour to convict her and again, Toni Jo asked for and won a new trial.

Her third trial happened in January 1942. Once more, the jury convicted her and, predictably, Toni Jo appealed on the grounds Louisiana had changed its execution method from hanging to the electric chair during her trials. But the Supreme Court ruled it constitutional and the governor signaled his eagerness to carry out the sentence.

After three trials and three convictions, Toni Jo Henry was sent to the Lake Charles prison to await her own death.

A FEW MONTHS BEFORE HER EXECUTION DATE, she decided to "kick the lid off" by granting a death-house interview to a local reporter. She spoke casually and smoked as she balanced a chair against the steel bars of her cell, revealing a more thoughtful side to the *femme fatale* she played proudly.

"Most folks wonder what goes on in the mind of a condemned person," she said. "In the first place, the victim doesn't return to haunt me. I don't think of him. I've known all along it would be my life for his. I believe mine is worth as much to me as his was to him. I wonder, though, sometimes, why it's legal now for some fellow to kill me."

Toni Jo rued that she might be electrocuted before she knew how a popular radio serial, "Abie's Irish Rose," would end. The reporter noted she had a faint Spanish accent, which Toni Jo attributed to her Texas days.

And the mere mention of Texas set her musing about Cowboy.

"I was a bad girl at 13, a drug addict at 16," she said. "Nobody ever cared about me before him. That guy is the king of my heart. He gave me a home and he got that drug monkey off my back.

"I remember the day I told him I was a cokie and the look on his face. He thought I just smoked marijuana and grinned. But when I told him my train went a lot further than marijuana he took me to a hotel room and I lay there in bed for a week and he would come in now and then and ask me how I was doing. He'd slap my face with iced towels and we'd both laugh."

No longer the Tigress, Toni Jo grew downright sentimental, in her way.

She'd married Cowboy, she said, because he was "the only man who ever treated me decent."

"The nights here are mean. Sometimes I pray he can get a letter through to me. He's smart. He's no Luke McGluke from Kokomo, that one. They say some condemned prisoners get a lot of grace from eating all the things they want just before they go, but me—I'd rather read a letter from him."

She ruminated about her life behind bars.

"I think condemned persons fret more about losing contact with human beings than anything else. You feel so out of it. It's more than these bars: it's more like a hellish battle with long distance when she won't give you a number—anybody's number—not one friendly human being's number. You get so cold and pretty soon you're a freak even to yourself."

But when the reporter asked about Joe Calloway, the unlucky Samaritan who left behind a wife and daughter, the Tigress returned.

"I've asked myself a thousand times and I don't know

why I killed that man," she said. "Sometimes I wonder why I didn't knock the man unconscious, but it was like being drunk, real drunk. I always knew there was a God running the show, but I thought maybe I could steal just one little act."

She admitted to the reporter that she, not the hapless Arkie Burks, had shot Calloway (and she signed a sworn affidavit confessing to be the trigger woman), although it merely confirmed what people had believed all along. Burks himself awaited death just a few cells down the row.

Before the interview ended, a photographer fiddled with his bulky camera while Toni Jo posed impatiently for some of her last photos.

"I've smiled twice, mister, and you haven't shot yet," she scolded. "Have you any idea how much talent is being wasted here today?"

JUST FIVE DAYS BEFORE TONI JO'S DATE WITH THE ELECTRIC CHAIR, Cowboy busted out of the prison farm at Sugarland, Texas, with a foolhardy scheme to spring her: He planned to kidnap the judge who sentenced her to die and hold him hostage until Toni Jo was freed.

He got as far as Beaumont, Texas, where cops busted him in a Crockett Street flophouse two days after his escape. Ironically, it was November 25, the second anniversary of his marriage to Toni Jo.

Toni Jo was secretly charmed by Cowboy's daring plot, but as always, the Tigress never wanted to appear soft. Instead, she said she was glad the "fool" had been caught before he got himself killed.

Just thirty-three months after she shot Joseph Calloway in that frozen rice field, Toni Jo faced her last hours. A local priest received her back into the Catholic Church. She arranged for a black-and-white terrier puppy that she'd kept in her cell to be delivered to her niece in Shreveport. She asked that her black crepe dress—the only one she owned--be sent to the cleaners, because it wouldn't be right to die in a dirty, wrinkled outfit.

And there was one last request.

It wasn't to receive a sumptuous meal nor for the slightest delay. She didn't ask for forgiveness. She made no desperate plea to the governor to spare her life.

She only wanted to talk to Cowboy one last time.

At first, her request was denied. It broke the rules. Besides, Cowboy was in solitary confinement at a Texas prison himself, and even if the warden had seriously considered it, there was no time to transport him safely to Louisiana to satisfy a killer's final romantic wish.

But the pending execution of a woman was a rare event in Louisiana—it had happened only twice before, so the sheriff bent the rules. He would allow a brief phone conversation.

The phone call from the chief jailer's office was brief. Toni Jo did most of the talking, and Cowboy just listened, sobbing.

"I know it has to come and I'm ready for it, honey," she told Cowboy. "I'm glad to have known you for the short time that I did. I'm sorry that things had to turn out this way. But you've got to live right, Claude. Go out the front door of that prison and get rid of that zoot suit [prison uniform] so your mother will be proud of you."

Her last wish granted, Toni Jo's call ended with a last wish for Cowboy.

"Go straight and try to make something of your life," she said, then hung up forever.

TONI JO DIDN'T SLEEP ON THE LAST NIGHT OF HER LIFE.

She refused a final meal. Her priest gave her last communion. She manicured her nails in silence. Her black crepe dress came back from the cleaners, pressed and perfect. She had promised not to make a fuss.

Louisiana's portable electric chair had been trucked in overnight from the prison in Angola and it waited just below Toni Jo's second-floor cell.

She cried—maybe for the first time—when a jailer came to shave her head just before she was led to the death chamber. The flowing, raven hair that had captivated so many reporters was shorn, and Toni Jo wrapped a flowered scarf around her bald head, knowing news photographers and a curious crowd had gathered outside.

Six minutes after noon on November 28, 1942, Toni Jo descended the stairs from her cellblock to the temporary death chamber below. Accompanied by her priest and the warden, she tightly clasped a small, white handkerchief in her left hand as flashbulbs popped. She was bare-legged, but wore black pumps. She wanted to look good. She even managed a smile for them.

Inside the death chamber, she sat primly in the electric chair, ignoring the official witnesses. The sheriff asked her if she had any last words and she replied quietly, "No."

She smiled at the executioner as he affixed the electrodes to her body, and murmured something to him that nobody could hear.

When he finished his grim work, she asked for the priest. While he stood before her and prayed, Toni Jo's fingers traced across a simple flower brooch she wore on her dress. She whispered something to the sheriff, and everyone stepped back.

The executioner untied the scarf around Toni Jo's

shaven head and replaced it with a metal skull-cap.

"Goodbye, Toni Jo," he said.

On a signal from the sheriff, the executioner flipped a switch. A low hum rose and fell away. Toni Jo's body trembled as 2,350 volts coursed through her. A wisp of smoke rose from her head. It was over in a few seconds.

Her corpse was loaded into a hearse and driven slowly away from the jail. The mortuary laid her body in a plain gray casket, in the simple black dress in which she'd died. Almost 8,000 gawkers came to see her, but not her family or Cowboy.

Toni Jo Henry was the first and last woman to die in Louisiana's electric chair, and only the third woman to be executed there. Louisiana hasn't executed a woman since then.

Nobody claimed her body, so she was buried at Lake Charles' Orange Grove Cemetery in a pauper's grave with a crucifix in her hand, as she had requested. She was 26.

Arkie Burks died in the same electric chair four months later, even though he hadn't killed Calloway. He walked to his death smiling and waving to friends in the crowd. Likewise, nobody claimed his body, so he was buried in an unmarked grave.

THE LOVE STORY DIDN'T END THERE, THOUGH.

When Cowboy got the news that Toni Jo was dead, he didn't cry, but he fell into a dark malaise and grew ill. Two years later, he was paroled. Too old to box anymore and plagued by a bad heart, he drifted into an ex-con's life in Dallas, but never got over his love for Toni Jo.

On July 14, 1945—just three months after he was paroled—Cowboy celebrated his thirty-second birthday at a seedy Dallas bar called the White Rock Inn. The night grew long, and Cowboy got drunker. Sometime after midnight, he demanded another drink but the bartender refused to serve him.

Angry and soused, Cowboy threatened to get a gun and blow the bartender's head off. He left the bar and returned a few minutes later, gun in hand.

The bartender didn't wait to see what this convicted killer would do next. He pulled a shotgun from under the bar and blasted Cowboy into eternity.

David Claude "Cowboy" Henry was buried in a family cemetery in his old hometown south of San Antonio, 350 miles away.

In the end, death was the prison from which they couldn't spring each other.

Photo Archive I

Toni Jo Henry just weeks before her historic 1942 execution in St. Charles.

Toni Jo, Thrill Slayer, Dies In Electric Chair

'Tiger Woman' Walks Unaided To Death Chamber After Weeping; Smiles At Her Executioner

By BICKNELL EUBANKS
United Press Staff Correspondent

LAKE CHARLES, La., Nov. 28.—Toni Jo Henry died in Louisiana's portable electric chair today.

Thus, the 26-year-old "tiger woman" who shot J. P. Calloway, a salesman, to death in a frozen rice field as he plead for his life, became the first woman to be electrocuted by the state of Louisiana.

As the lethal current smashed through her fragile body, her accomplice in murder, Horace Finnon Burks, sat shivering in his cell a few yards away from the death chamber.

Only last week Toni Jo signed a statement taking full responsibility for Calloway's death, which Burks plans to use in an appeal from his death sentence.

Makes No Statement

Accompanied by Father Richard [illegible], her spiritual advisor, and prison officials Toni Jo descended the stairs from the second floor cell bloc at 12:[illegible] p. m.

Ten minutes later she was dead.

Pale, but controlling herself well, she made no last statement.

When Sheriff Henry Reid Jr., asked her if she had any last word, she replied: "No."

Then she smiled at the executioner, as he fixed the electrodes to her body.

[illegible] shaved of the lustrous, raven hair of which she was so proud, was covered by a flowered kerchief.

She held a small white handkerchief in her tightly clasped left

Toni Jo Henry's execution made national headlines.

CONVICT HUBBY OF TONI JO IS AGAIN HUNTED

Cowboy Henry Escapes Prison; May Attempt To Save Wife

Lake Charles, La., Nov. 24 (AP) —Law enforcement officers were ready today for Claude E. (Cowboy) Henry, escaped Texas convict, if he should come here to try to spring his doomed wife from the Calcasieu parish jail.

"All necessary precautions have been taken," said Sheriff Henry Reid, Jr., when notified the 29-

Readers briefly held their breath when a desperate Cowboy Henry escaped days before his condemned wife's date with the electric chair.

DEATH FROM ABOVE

Howard Johnson Hotel Sniper, New Orleans 1973

A COLD SKY, WATER-COLORED IN SHADES OF GRAY, HUNG LOW over the parish voting hall on Election Day.

Tim Ursin hunkered into his coat and inched along in the long line outside, trying to keep warm. The brisk wind carried a hint of Gulf salt. He'd spent his whole life in these bayous, going on sixty-six years now, and he loved the water, but today wasn't a good day for fishing. Today was for voting. A black man talking about hope looked like he might win this historic presidential election, not just for Louisiana, but for the country and maybe the world.

"Cold one today," said the young African-American man in his mid-thirties in line ahead of him. He turned his back to the wind, facing Tim.

"It is."

"Line's movin', but I wish it was movin' faster."

"Got nothin' else to do today," Tim said. "Can't fish."

"I hear ya," the man said. "I love to fish, but today just ain't the day."

The young man introduced himself to Tim. He was a truck driver with a family.

"What do you do?" he asked.

"I'm a fishing guide," Tim said. He reached in his pocket for a business card and the young man saw the silvery steel hook where his left hand once was.

"I hope you won't be offended," the curious man said, "but what happened to your hand?"

Tim smiled. People always wanted to know about the hook, even if they didn't ask. He was used to it. And, hell, he'd told the story so many times in the past thirty-five years, he didn't mind telling it again.

"It's okay. I was a firefighter. I've been retired from the New Orleans Fire Department since '75. I was shot a long time ago, in '73, by a sniper at the Howard Johnson. Lost my arm up to here," he said, wrapping his good right hand around the stump of his left forearm.

The young man's eyes flickered with recognition as Tim told about another cold morning in New Orleans when he crossed paths with a killer.

"I heard about that guy! I was just a little kid, but my parents talked about it," he said. He stumbled slightly over his next words: "He was   he was a black guy, wasn't he?"

"Yeah, but he " Tim started to say.

"I'm sorry, man. I mean, that you were shot by a   a black man."

"Hey, you didn't do it," Tim assured him. "I appreciate that, but you don't have to be sorry or feel bad for what somebody else did. Didn't matter what color he was then, and doesn't now."

"Thanks, man," he said. "But if it happened to me, I just don't know how I couldn't be bitter   "

They talked about the shooting as long as they could. Inside the voting area, they parted ways in front of the poll workers' table.

"I admire you," the young truck driver said. "I mean, the way you look at it."

"Life goes on," Tim said. "Doesn't do any good to dwell on something that happened a long time ago, you know?

Everything has a purpose. Every day's a gift. You just never know. I just gotta keep moving forward and not just for me, but for the people around me, too."

The man smiled, shook Tim's hand, and was gone.

It's funny, Tim thought, how the murky water of memory gets churned up on cold mornings.

A CHILLY DRIZZLE FELL ALL NIGHT ON NEW ORLEANS. For a few hours between the last late-night jazz riffs in the Quarter and the first peal of St. Louis Cathedral's bells, the only sound was rain. The Sunday morning streets, absolved of Saturday night, lay greasy blue and empty under leaden January skies.

Before dawn on January 7, 1973, Lieutenant Tim Ursin kissed his wife and three sleeping children goodbye and arrived at New Orleans Fire Department Station Fourteen a little before 7 a.m. He was only twenty-nine but already a nine-year firehouse veteran and one of the NOFD's most promising young officers, maybe even a future district chief. He'd spent part of his rookie year at Engine Fourteen, as it was known in the department, and now was coming back to help out his short-handed buddies.

Engine Fourteen was a busy station near the center of New Orleans, surrounded by Charity Hospital, City Hall, downtown hotels, some dreary ghetto housing and projects, and one of New Orleans' forty-two cemeteries, where big rainstorms had been known to pop airtight caskets right out of the waterlogged earth like macabre bubbles. In New Orleans, death and water have always had an uneasy kinship.

But Tim loved New Orleans, the city where he was born. His father had played drums with the great Pete Fountain and some of the Dixieland bands that set the rhythm for the beating heart of the Crescent City. He'd met his wife here and was raising three kids here, too. It had everything he ever wanted, and he never needed to leave. Sure, there was crime, pervasive corruption, decadence, and dreadful poverty, but the city hid it all behind a mask of Old World architecture and sumptuous menus of bayou cuisine, iron-lace balconies, and endless revelry.

Rainy, winter Sundays were usually slow for firefighters, so Tim spent the morning helping with mundane chores around the station, sweeping floors, making beds, and washing the trucks. Because nobody cooked on leisurely Sundays, the firefighters usually ordered takeout.

Tim was the extra man today, so he volunteered to make a lunch run to a local burger joint a couple blocks away. He took everybody's order and was heading to his car when somebody hollered for him to wait while they called another local place to see if they had hot lunches. When nobody answered, he turned to leave, but the firehouse radio beeped twice—the signal for a working fire with visible smoke someplace in the city.

"Engines Sixteen, Fourteen Twenty-seven, Truck Eight, Three-Oh-Two," a dispatcher blared at 10:45 a.m. "Go to Howard Johnson Motor Court, Three-Three-Zero Loyola. Working fire."

The Howard Johnson was just two minutes from Engine Fourteen, damn near a straight shot. Firefighters scrambled as Tim quickly yanked on his bunker gear and grabbed a jump seat behind the pumper's cab.

As they pulled up in front of the seventeen-story high-rise hotel, Tim saw black smoke belching from windows on the eighth or ninth floor. This was no mattress fire.

Worse, just six weeks before, a mysterious arson fire

had swept through the top three floors of the seventeen-story Rault Center—a luxury office and apartment complex right next door to the Howard Johnson—killing six. Five had leapt to their deaths from fifteenth-floor windows because the firefighters couldn't pump water high enough and had no ladders tall enough to rescue them. The New Orleans' Fire Department had reason to be edgy about another skyscraper fire.

Truck Eight, an aerial-ladder truck, pulled up in front of the hotel just ahead of Engine Fourteen, a water pumper. The operator was already setting his stabilizer jacks so he could extend his ladder to snatch frantic hotel guests who were already screaming from upper-floor balconies. But even if he were perfectly positioned, his ladder would only reach the ninth floor. Visions of the Rault Center were already starting to sweep through the firefighters on the ground.

A district fire chief grabbed Tim amid the chaos of running firefighters, civilians, and cops.

"Come with me," he barked. "Let's see what we've got here."

They entered the hotel's lobby as frightened guests streamed down stairwells from their rooms above. Anxious to know exactly what they faced, Tim instantly made a plan: he'd take an elevator up to the sixth or seventh floor, then scramble up the stairs to the fire above. He grabbed two firefighters and started for the elevator but was quickly stopped by armed cops.

"Can't go up there," they said. "We got a guy with a shotgun trapped in the elevator and we're trying to get him out."

Blocked from the stairs, too, Tim went back outside. Truck Eight sat empty, its crew working elsewhere. Its stabilizers were set, but there was nobody to operate its ladder.

Except Tim Ursin. He had trained on Truck Eight and knew how to deploy its life-saving, hundred-foot ladder.

He leapt up to the console on the back of the truck and began to maneuver the ladder into position, swinging it around toward the burning hotel, then extending it slowly to just below ninth-floor balcony where he saw people yelling and waving hysterically. Some already had their legs over the railings, ready to jump. The whole operation might have taken four minutes, but it seemed like a lifetime to Tim.

Once the ladder was in place, he looked around. Firefighters were dashing everywhere but none were ready to go up.

"I can't wait around," he shouted to a cop nearby. "I'm going up. Gimme that wash-out line."

Tim stuck his right arm through the coiled inch-and-a-half line—a sixty-pound hose that he could plug into to a standpipe in the hotel's internal fire suppression system—and stepped onto the ladder.

"Here's your belt," a passing firefighter said, tossing up the safety strap commonly used in ladder rescues. Tim would be more than eighty feet up, standing on the wet, narrow steps of a flexing ladder, wrestling with panic-stricken people.

"Ain't gonna use it," Tim said as he started up. "I'm going straight up and not stopping."

As he climbed, the wash-out hose's five-pound brass nozzle slapped against the back of his knee, slowing him down. He paused at the seventh floor and told the people on the balcony twenty feet above to calm down. Steadying himself with his left hand on the rung at eye level, he reached behind his leg with his right hand and grabbed the dangling nozzle, which he tucked between his chin and left shoulder.

A loud bang erupted somewhere off to Tim's left. The shock jolted his left arm as he reached up the hand rail, and he felt a soft rush of heat ripple across his face.

Somebody up there is tossing cherry bombs, he thought. *These people could die and they're playing with fireworks?*

Then his left arm began to burn, just a little at first. He looked down at the heavy sleeve of his fire coat to see lumpy gore spilling out, as if someone had opened a bloody faucet.

Tim quickly pivoted, turning his back to the ladder. He tried to gather his wits, but he could literally feel his blood pressure dropping. He didn't know what had happened, but he could tell from the thick flow of blood and the searing pain that he'd been hurt badly, and he wasn't sure he'd make it to the ground alive.

Stay awake! he commanded himself. *If you fall, you die.*

He started down the ladder on his heels, steadying himself with his good hand.

He began to shout, to firefighters below, to the people above, to God to anybody who could hear his act of contrition.

My God, I am sorry for my sins with all my heart...

His left arm seemed to be on fire, as if someone had jammed a white-hot poker up his sleeve into the soft flesh of his forearm.

in choosing to do wrong and failing to do good

He saw cops with rifles and handguns below, shooting up toward him. He realized he was caught in some kind of crossfire.

I have sinned against you whom I should love above all

things

Could anyone hear? He wanted people to know he'd confessed his sins before he died up there.

I firmly intend, with your help, to do penance, to sin no more, and to avoid whatever leads me to sin

Growing woozy, Tim saw his friend Huey Brown, a beefy tillerman on the ladder truck, hurrying up the ladder.

"I'm coming up to get you!" Brown yelled.

"No, get down!" Tim yelled back. "He's gonna shoot you, too."

Brown kept coming.

"Fuck it!" he shouted.

Brown reached Tim and wedged his brawny shoulders under the wounded fireman's legs. Rung by slow rung, he eased Tim the last twenty feet down the precarious ladder, knowing somebody was up above them with a gun. Tim's gushing blood streamed over Brown's helmet, his shoulders, his face, and hands as he lowered his comrade to safety.

A New Orleans cop met Brown at the bottom of the ladder, while another officer covered them with a shotgun. They lowered Tim's body off the fire truck's rear turntable to a safe spot on the pavement behind Engine Fourteen, out of the line of fire.

A fireman cut off Tim's heavy coat, exposing a gaping wound that looked like it was inflicted by a dull pickaxe on the meaty part of his left forearm. The bullet had passed completely through, shattering bone and nearly sawing his arm off completely. The fireman wrapped Tim's black leather, NOFD-issue belt with a shiny silver buckle around Tim's upper arm to stanch the bleeding before they loaded him in an ambulance.

AT CHARITY HOSPITAL'S EMERGENCY ROOM, NURSES

PUSHED HIS GURNEY against the wall as more shooting victims rolled in behind him. The place was pandemonium. The wounded were crying and moaning as overwhelmed doctors and nurses rushed around. Cops and firefighters scurried among them all, confused and in shock. Blood stained everything.

Tim fought the worsening pain. He begged for painkillers, but nobody was listening. They couldn't give him anything until they knew the precise extent of his wounds.

Orderlies finally rolled Tim into an examination room, where he was transferred onto the cold, bare stainless steel table beneath a bright light. He was fading fast. Except for the blinding light over him, the rest of the room appeared to be dark. Ghostly figures worked all around him, removed his clothes, searched for more wounds, probed his butchered arm, emptied blood from his boots, and murmured in uneasy tones words he couldn't understand.

The bullet had blown away a biscuit-sized chunk of Tim's arm flesh and smashed his radius, one of the two bones in his forearm. It severed his radial nerve and ruptured both arteries in his left arm. He had already lost more than three pints of blood, about one-third of his life fluid.

As he floated at the brink of consciousness, a prayer rose above the pain. Then a hand from the darkness daubed his forehead, eyes, and lips with oil, and made the sign of the cross over him.

" May the Lord pardon thee whatever sins or faults thou hast committed "

He knew the voice. It was Father Pete Rogers, the fire department's chaplain. He was giving last rites.

" I grant you a plenary indulgence for the remission of

all your sins, and I bless you. In the name of the Father and the Son and the Holy Spirit   "

It was the last thing that Tim wanted to hear. He wasn't even thirty. He had three kids and a wife. He didn't want to die. He wasn't ready.

He didn't know that God or destiny or maybe just dumb luck had already intervened to save his life. The 240-grain, .44 Magnum bullet that mangled his left arm had passed completely through the thick sleeve of his fire coat and lodged in the annoying brass hose nozzle he had just tucked under his chin. It had stopped the slug from tearing into his neck.

And he didn't know that the sniper took aim at him a second time, but maybe by the same trick of providence or fluke, his gun didn't fire.

Tim drifted into unconsciousness on the table. The next thing he remembered was waking up in a dark hospital room. He heard moaning and solemn voices he didn't recognize. In a few hours, he learned there were three gravely wounded cops with him there in the dark: Officer Skeets Palmisano had been shot in the back and the arm as he ran across a grassy mall in front of the hotel; Patrolman Chuck Arnold had been shot in the face as he stood in the window of an office building across from the hotel, and although his jaw was nearly gone, he had walked a few blocks to the nearest hospital; Officer Ken Solis was trying to keep onlookers back when a single bullet blew a massive hole in his right shoulder and his belly.

Tim could hear something else. Not in the room but somewhere outside in the night. Distant but chilling.

He could hear gunfire.

THE FIRST SHOTS WERE FIRED A WEEK EARLIER, ON NEW

YEAR'S EVE, 1972, although some would argue later that this war began centuries before.

A phantom gunman lay in wait in a vacant lot across from New Orleans' Central Lockup on Perdido Street—where prisoners are booked, fingerprinted, and photographed—just before the jail's 11 p.m. shift change. When two police recruits came into view, he cut loose with seven shots from a high-powered rifle, killing nineteen-year-old unarmed police cadet Alfred Harrell and wounding a lieutenant.

Police searching the empty lot found a dropped .38-caliber blue-steel Colt revolver, spent .44 Magnum shell casings, footprints, several strings of firecrackers, and other evidence left by the shooter, but he had melted into the night.

But eighteen minutes later, another cop, thirty-year-old K-9 officer Ed Hosli, was mortally wounded while investigating a burglar alarm less than a quarter-mile from the jail at a warehouse in Gert Town, a poor, black neighborhood where crime and hatred of cops flourished. Spent casings and other evidence at the scene—including a leather bag containing two cans of lighter fluid and some firecrackers—pointed to the same assailant who shot up the city lockup.

The next day, when police flooded Gert Town looking for the assailant, they were treated as an invading enemy. Armed black men shadowed the cops. NOPD switchboards were swamped with callers reporting dozens of fake sniper sightings. After nightfall, some locals shot out streetlights, making the investigation harder and adding an element of menace.

Even before the New Year's Eve shootings, tensions between New Orleans cops and the city's poor blacks had been high. In the past year, Police Superintendent Clarence Giarrusso had created the Felony Action Squad, an elite unit assigned to target violence in the city's most crime-ridden neighborhoods. Announcing the squad's formation in 1972, Giarrusso proudly told reporters that if any of the unit's twelve undercover agents encountered armed robbers, rapists, or murderers, they could "shoot to kill."

A series of armed conflicts with Black Panthers and several other black revolutionary organizations in New Orleans's Desire public housing projects only made matters worse.

Louisiana was smoldering with racial friction. The previous January, two Black Muslim militants were shot to death by police at a Baton Rouge race riot in which two white deputies also died; among the thirty-one wounded, fourteen were cops. And on November 16, 1972, two black student protesters were shot and killed at Southern University in Baton Rouge, but their killer (allegedly a police officer) was never identified.

So when the Gert Town sweep wrapped up, the NOPD had precious few clues to their sniper's identity or whereabouts. It was clear that the same shooter (or shooters) shot three cops on New Year's Eve, probably with the same .44 Magnum rifle. They also knew he had wounded himself while trying to break into the warehouse because he left a trail of bloody handprints and spatters.

But the investigation wasn't dead by a long shot. One bit of evidence looked like a promising piece of the puzzle.

A young, slightly built black man had broken into a black Baptist church in Gert Town the night of the shootings. When he was surprised by the pastor the next day, he fled, leaving a satchel of bullets, bloodstains all around the sanctuary, and an apology: "I am sorry for breaking the lock on your church door but pastor at two o'clock I felt I had to get right with the Lord. You see I was a sinner then walking past your church   I was drinking   I then broke the door and fell on my knees in prayer. Now I have managed to get it together. I will send you the money for a new lock. God bless you."

And some potential clues were never fully investigated or simply missed.

Two days after the shootings, a local grocer named Joe Perniciaro told police a young black man with a bloody bandage on his left hand had come into his store just a couple blocks from the warehouse where Hosli was shot. The kid wore a dark jacket and Army fatigues, and Perniciaro feared he might rob the place, but he left without incident after buying a razor.

On Perdido Street, just two blocks from Central Lockup, patrolmen found an abandoned two-door, blue 1963 Chevrolet with Kansas plates and the keys still in the ignition. When they ran the license number, LYE 1367, it came back to a Mark James Robert Essex, age twenty-four, of 902 Cottonwood Street in Emporia, Kansas. With no priors and no warrants, the kid checked out, so police wrote it off as a stalled vehicle and cleared young Essex.

But before the New Year's Eve sniper investigation could unfold fully, before New Orleans could rest easier, even before the coming week was finished   a bloody, one-man race war would erupt in the worst carnage the city had seen since the War of 1812.

And police would hear the name Mark Essex again.

THE PRIVATE WAR OF MARK JAMES ESSEX BEGAN IN THE PEACEFUL PRAIRIE TOWN of Emporia, Kansas, an American Gothic village once described as "grassland, stoplights, grassland again."

Emporia was a meat-packing town of fewer than thirty thousand citizens, but fewer than five hundred of them were black in the 1960s. Jimmy—as his friends and family called him—was the second of five children born to Nellie and Mark Henry Essex, a foreman at one of the local meat plants. The seven of them lived in a modest white frame house on the eastern edge of town, near the Santa Fe Railroad tracks, where most of the town's minorities also lived.

Jimmy grew up happy but soft-spoken, congenial but unremarkable. He was the kid nobody noticed and few remembered. He loved to fish and hunt, and he was a crack shot. He attended church faithfully enough that he talked about becoming a minister someday. He mowed neighbors' lawns for pocket money. Jimmy Essex was, both literally and metaphorically, a Boy Scout and a choirboy, not a loner or rebel.

In school, Jimmy was a C student who probably had Bs in him, but he never pushed himself that hard. Short and skinny, he didn't play sports, although he played saxophone in the Emporia Senior High School band for three years. When it appeared he was better with his hands than with his mind, Jimmy spent his last two years at a vocational-technical school, where he focused on auto mechanics.

In January 1969, after one listless semester at college and worries over being drafted to fight in Vietnam, Jimmy Essex enlisted for four years in the U.S. Navy. After graduating from boot camp with outstanding ratings, he went to dental technician school, where he graduated with the highest honors before being assigned to the clinic at the naval air station in Imperial Beach, California.

Jimmy wasn't in Kansas anymore. Back home, he'd

never seen racism as virulent as he saw in the Navy, where he came to believe black men were still treated as second-class citizens. He suffered racial slurs, ridiculous and meticulous searches of his car when he came and went from the base, harassment in the barracks, extra guard duty, trifling orders from white superiors intended only to exasperate—all irritations that most black sailors encountered but shrugged off.

But not Jimmy Essex.

Although only five-foot-four and less than one hundred forty pounds, Jimmy fought back physically. Sometimes he complained bitterly to officers about the racist behavior he experienced. In letters home, he wrote that "blacks have trouble getting along here." His constant skirmishing often landed him in trouble and marked him as a troublemaker.

Eventually, Jimmy befriended a black sailor named Rodney Frank, a convicted rapist and armed robber from New Orleans who hid behind his own militant bombast. Frank introduced Jimmy to radical Black Panther literature, to the revolutionary writings of Eldridge Cleaver and Huey Newton, and to Black Muslim fanatics off-base.

In a matter of months, everything changed. Jimmy Essex, the quiet choirboy from Kansas, was dead. Mark Essex, the angry revolutionary, stood defiantly in his place.

On October 19, 1970, Essex went AWOL. He packed a duffel bag and boarded a bus back home to Emporia. When his parents picked him up at the bus depot, he told them he'd come home "to think about what a black man has to do to survive."

He was angry, bitter, and isolated, obsessed with the wrongs he'd suffered and adamant about not returning to the Navy. His worried mother asked the Rev. W.A. Chambers, the Baptist minister who'd baptized Jimmy at age twelve, to speak to her son. Essex wanted to hear none of it. He was not only disillusioned with the world, but with God, too.

"Christianity is a white man's religion," he told his former minister, "and the white man's been running things too long."

Twenty-eight days later, Essex returned to his base to face a court-martial.

Although he had already pleaded guilty to being absent without leave, Essex's defense was that the Navy's entrenched racism was to blame. Hate made him do it. "I had to talk to some black people because I had begun to hate all white people. I was tired of going to white people and telling them my problems and not getting anything done about it."

The court actually gave credence to Essex's claims of discrimination and handed out a relatively insignificant sentence, but within weeks, Essex was given a special discharge for unspecified "character and behavior disorders" after a Navy psychiatrist had concluded that Essex had an "immature personality." In his report, the psychiatrist noted that Essex exhibited no suicidal tendencies but "he alludes to the fact he 'might do something' if he doesn't get what he wants."

In the end, the Navy washed its hands of Seaman Mark James Essex, who served little more than half his enlistment.

Starting in February 1971, Essex spent a few months in New York City, where he voraciously consumed Black Panther Party propaganda and fueled the flames that were beginning to flicker deep inside. He studied the Panthers' urban guerilla warfare tactics and started calling cops "pigs." He also learned that one of the Panthers' weapons of choice was the .44 Magnum semiautomatic carbine, a light and powerful hunting rifle that was devastating at close range.

Back in Emporia, Essex couldn't adjust. His few childhood friends had all moved away, and he yearned to live in a black man's city. He worked a series of odd jobs for a year or so but never with any enthusiasm. His hatred, though, continued to simmer.

Then one day, he walked into the local Montgomery Ward store and bought himself a .44 Magnum Ruger Deerslayer rifle, which he practiced firing in the countryside until the gun had become an extension of him.

Whether Emporia had become too claustrophobic or Essex had decided to launch a new front in his private race war, nobody knows. But in the summer of 1972, he picked up the phone, called his old friend Rodney Frank—also recently drummed out of the Navy as an incorrigible—and decided to move to New Orleans.

To the outside world, Mark Essex appeared to be just another young black man who didn't know exactly where he was going or why. He entered a training program for vending-machine repairmen and rented a cheap apartment in the back of a shabby house.

But inwardly, he was reaching an ugly kind of critical mass. His defiant, revolutionary outlook grew darker. He began calling himself Mata, the Swahili word for a hunter's bow. He was devouring militant newspapers and books. And he was filling every inch of the pale brown walls in his little two-room with a hateful scrawl of angry anti-white slogans like "My death lies in the bloody death of racist pigs," "Political power comes from the barrel of a gun," "Hate white people beast of the earth," "Kill pig Nixon and all his running dogs."

All references to whites, and that was most of them, were daubed in red paint. The rest were black. He even wrote on the ceiling, taunting the police he knew would eventually visit his frowzy sanctuary: "Only a pig would read shit on the ceiling."

In November 1972, when Essex heard the news that two black students had been gunned down at Southern University while protesting the white man's oppression, he declared his own personal war on whites and cops.

After Christmas, he hand-wrote a note to a local TV station announcing his bloody intentions:

> *Africa greets you.*
>
> *On Dec. 31, 1972, aprx. 11 pm, the downtown New Orleans Police Department will be attacked. Reason — many, but the death of two innocent brothers will be avenged. And many others.*
>
> *P.S. Tell pig Giarrusso the felony action squad ain't shit.*
> *MATA*

The attack happened as Essex had promised, although the letter was not opened at the TV station until days later. It was revealed too late to prevent the murders of Alfred Harrell and Ed Hosli. Nevertheless, it would not only link Mark Essex undeniably to those New Year's Eve shootings—in which his first victim, ironically, was a black man—but foretold a bigger, bloodier butchery to come.

ON THE RAIN-SHROUDED MORNING OF SUNDAY, JANUARY 7, 1973, Mark Essex girded for battle.

Almost a thousand miles away, Nellie Essex prepared for church, where she would cry and pray for her son's wayward soul.

Tim Ursin kissed his children goodbye before going to work.

And a whole city awoke to a misty, gray day that would be unlike any before it.

Shortly after 10 a.m., Mark Essex walked back into Joe Perniciaro's market and stood in the doorway holding his .44 Magnum hunting rifle in his right hand. With his wounded left hand, he pointed at Perniciaro.

"You. You're the one I want," Essex shouted. "Come here."

Perniciaro recognized him as the bandaged young man who bought the razor five days before. He started to run toward the back of the store. Essex, believing Perniciaro had fingered him to the cops, had come for revenge.

Essex fired one booming shot, blasting a gaping hole in the grocer's right shoulder and knocking him to the floor before he turned and ran down the street.

Four blocks away, a fleeing Essex ran up to a black man sitting in front of his house in a beige-and-black 1968 Chevrolet Chevelle.

"Hi, brother, get out," Essex told him.

"You crazy, man?"

Essex leveled his rifle at the stunned man's head.

"I don't want to kill you, brother. Just honkies," he said calmly. "But I will kill you, too."

Jumping into the car, Essex peeled out in the stolen Chevelle, sideswiping another vehicle before disappearing into traffic.

Police radios crackled with nearly simultaneous reports of a shooting and an armed carjacking in the Gert Town district. Cruisers scrambled to respond, but the stolen Chevelle eluded them. All they had was a description of a slim, young black male, up to five-foot-four, weighing about a hundred forty pounds, wearing a green camouflage jacket and olive-drab fatigue pants. He was carrying a hunting rifle onto which he'd tied a red, green, and black handkerchief—later identified as the Black Liberation flag.

While police searched for the stolen Chevelle, Mark Essex careened into the parking garage of the Howard Johnson Hotel on Loyola Street and parked it on the fourth level. He ran up the stairwell to a locked fire door on the eighth floor, where he pounded until two black maids came to the door. He told one he wanted to visit a friend who was staying on the eighteenth floor.

She hesitated. She could lose her job if she let a stranger through the fire door.

"Are you a soul sister?" he asked one of them.

She said she was.

"Sister, the revolution is here," he said. "It's one for all and two for one."

But the maid still wouldn't let him enter, so Essex climbed another flight of stairs to the ninth floor, where he again pounded on the fire door and was again turned away by a maid.

On the eighteenth floor, he found a fire door propped open and went into the hallway, where he encountered two frightened maids and a houseman, all black.

"Don't worry, I'm not going to hurt you black people," he reassured them as he hurried past. "I want the whites."

But before Essex could get to an elevator, a white guest, twenty-seven-year-old Dr. Robert Steagall, saw him with the gun and tried to tackle him. They wrestled desperately for a few seconds before Essex shot the doctor in the chest. When Betty Steagall ran to her husband's aid, Essex coolly put the muzzle of his carbine against the base of her skull and pulled the trigger. She died embracing her dead husband.

Essex untied the Black Liberation flag from his gun and threw it near their corpses.

Inside the Steagalls' room, Essex set their drapes on fire and ran to the nearest stairwell.

Moving quickly throughout the hotel, he started several fires on various floors by soaking phone books with lighter fluid, then igniting them beneath the draperies. The whole time, he'd shoot at any white folks he saw and set off firecrackers in smoky halls and stairwells to create the illusion that many snipers and arsonists were prowling the hotel's eighteen floors, killing at random.

On the eleventh floor, he shot the hotel's assistant manager point-blank in the head, blowing most of it away. On the tenth floor, he mortally wounded the general manager. On the eighth-floor patio, a gut-shot hotel guest floated in the hotel pool for two hours, playing dead.

On the eighth floor, Essex heard sirens outside. From the balcony of one room, he saw a firefighter scrambling up an aerial ladder toward hysterical guests on the floor above. He took careful aim and squeezed the trigger, hitting the fireman. He racked another cartridge into the chamber and took aim again, but the gun didn't fire. He didn't have time for another shot. Cops on the ground were firing back, so he ducked for cover.

By 11 a.m., less than a half hour after Mark Essex laid siege to the Howard Johnson, police had set up a command center in the lobby, and hundreds of police surrounded the hotel. Sharpshooters had taken positions atop nearby buildings while other cops tried to keep curious onlookers out of the line of fire.

But it was fruitless. Local TV stations were going live, and their feeds were being picked up by networks for wall-to-wall coverage. Mark Essex's war was being televised.

Worse, word was leaking out that the snipers were militant black revolutionaries, and many angry African-Americans were gathering on the street outside the Howard Johnson to "Right on!" and "Kill the Pigs!" every time shots were fired from the balconies above.

From his perch on the eighth floor, Essex began to pick off cops who were scurrying in the streets below. One after another, they were falling wounded and dead.

In the meantime, some cops—led by the NOPD's second-in-command, Louis Sirgo—began to work their way through the choking black smoke into the bowels of the hotel, searching for what they believed were at least three snipers. In a darkened stairwell just above the sixteenth floor, Essex shot Sirgo in the spine almost point-blank, killing him.

For several hours, police exchanged fire with the phantom shooters, who continued to set fires. A circling police helicopter even took fire from the hotel. Descriptions of the shooters varied so widely that police were convinced they faced a small army of cold-blooded militants who held key strategic positions throughout the hotel. They were everywhere and nowhere.

At 3:30 p.m., police began securing the hotel, floor-by-floor, hoping ultimately to corner the snipers on the top floor, where fires were burning unabated.

Sometime around 4 p.m., more than five hours after the first shots were fired, police believed they had pushed the snipers onto the hotel's roof, where they had taken refuge in a concrete cubicle at the top of the stairwell and elevator shaft. It was a nearly impregnable bunker, especially since police were neither close enough nor armed with sufficiently powerful weapons to penetrate its thick walls.

Cops hiding in the stairwells below the cubicle could hear somebody moving around, cursing at sharpshooters on nearby buildings. "Africa! Africa!" he'd chant. At odd intervals, a sniper would run out on the graveled roof, fire several shots at police, then scamper back into his safe pillbox.

"Come on up, you honky pigs!" Essex yelled once as he fired down into the stairwell. "You afraid to fight like a black man?"

"Fuck you! Fuck you! Fuck you!" they screamed back. But all they could do was scream.

Even then, nobody knew exactly how many shooters were up there, how they were armed or how much ammo they had.

ONE OF THE MANY AMERICANS INTENTLY WATCHING THE VIOLENT DRAMA UNFOLD ON TELEVISION was Marine Lt. Colonel Chuck Pitman, a tough helicopter pilot who'd flown twelve hundred combat missions in Vietnam, been shot down seven times and won four Distinguished Flying Crosses. After the Rault fire, local Marines and Coast Guard chopper crews drew up contingency plans to help local police and fire departments in case of another high-rise fire. So where was the Coast Guard? Pitman wondered.

Fog, wind, and low skies made flying too dangerous, a Coast Guard commander told Pitman.

But Pitman knew the cops needed his help. At least seven people were dead and dozens wounded. The snipers had the high ground and the firepower to do even more damage.

"Shit," Pitman said. "It's not too bad for me. I can fly up the river."

Within an hour, Pitman and his crew were inching up the Mississippi River toward the city, sometimes only inches above the water. By 5:30, Pitman and three police marksmen were aloft in a twin-rotor military helicopter with shoot-to-kill orders. Incredibly, they were about to strafe the roof of a downtown hotel in an ordinary American city—but this was a war.

Over the next several hours, Pitman played a cat-and-mouse game with the shooters. Time after time, the chopper took fire until it rose over the roof, then nobody. The airborne police sharpshooters were pouring thousands of rounds into the concrete cubicle, but they couldn't see anyone. Yet, when the helicopter would move away, police observers on nearby buildings saw somebody run out and resume shooting.

Essex was hiding by climbing a water pipe and wedging himself under the bunker's ceiling. So when the chopper hovered above, police marksmen couldn't see him and their bullets ricocheted harmlessly all around him.

But once Pitman's crew figured it out, a simple tactic was employed. While a fire truck on the ground pumped water into the hotel's system, one of Pitman's sharpshooters poured a stream of tracer bullets into the pressurized pipe. It exploded.

Cops on the chopper unleashed a ferocious storm of fire on the cubicle. Forced from his hiding place by a spewing pipe and flying concrete chips, Essex ran from the cubicle holding his rifle and looked straight up at Pitman.

He yelled something nobody heard and raised his fist in one last defiant act before he was slaughtered in a hail of gunfire.

A little before 9 p.m., Mark Essex lay dead on the roof of the Howard Johnson, but the war wasn't finished. Police kept firing into his body without mercy, and they shot his rifle into bits so none of his accomplices could use it. Throughout the night, police radioed that other snipers were shooting at them, or saw gun flashes in the dark, or heard taunts from hidden corners of the hotel.

And they watched the phantom corpse of Mark Essex all night. An occasional night breeze would sometimes flutter through the shreds of his fatigues or his black turtleneck sweater and they would swear he was still alive. Somebody would shoot him again, just to be sure.

The next morning, after the sun had risen, cops stormed the roof and found only Mark Essex's ruined body. It had been hit by more than two hundred bullets and was virtually unrecognizable. One leg was nearly severed. Pieces of him were scattered for yards around, including his jaw and tongue, which had been blasted across the roof. One witnesses said the body was so ravaged that "we nearly had to use a shovel to scoop him up."

Essex's racist rampage was among the worst mass shooting in American history, even if it fell out of the public consciousness unusually quickly. Firing more than a hundred shots, Essex had killed nine people and wounded ten more. Five of the dead and five of the wounded were police officers. Of Essex's nineteen victims, only one was black.

To this day, some cops believe with all their hearts that there were other snipers, but the official police ruling was that Mark Essex acted alone. Police found no metal casings that matched any other gun but Essex's .44 Magnum carbine.

Nevertheless, the Rault Center arson fire six weeks before is now generally believed to have been a dry run for Essex's attack at the Howard Johnson. If true, his death toll would rise to a grim fifteen innocent people.

Black outrage erupted within hours of Essex's death.

EVEN BEFORE ESSEX'S BODY HAD BEEN SHIPPED BACK TO EMPORIA in a simple wooden crate, black militant leader Stokely Carmichael praised Essex for "carrying our struggle to the next quantitative level, the level of science."

And within days, columnist Phil Smith of the *Chicago Metro News*, an activist black weekly, eulogized Essex as a "new hero in an old struggle."

"Essex may not have been in love with white people, but that made him as normal as 30 million other Black people," Smith wrote.

He suggested Essex was framed by a "sick white racist society" bent on the "systematic extermination of young Black men." No young black man, he said, would ever "go berserk and kill white people for no reason."

"White people hate the idea that Black people, by virtue of their very existence, force whites to deal with their own dishonesty, deceit and criminal intent   White people truly believe 'the only good nigger is a dead nigger,'" Smith seethed. "If there was one lesson that [Essex] had learned in his short life, it was that Black men are the most dispensable item in this country."

Even Essex's mother, resolute in her conviction that racism had transformed her cheerful little boy into a monster, was almost defiant when she spoke to reporters a week after the rampage.

"I do think Jimmy was driven to this," she said. "Jimmy was trying to make white America sit up and be aware of what is happening to us.

"I don't want my son to have died in vain," Mrs. Essex continued. "If this terrible thing will awaken white America to the injustices that blacks suffer, then some good will have come from it."

Although the Howard Johnson attack swiftly resurrected

the ghosts of Charles Whitman's 1966 Texas Tower massacre, it quickly fell out of the national media spotlight. Many observers believe stories about black rage ran counter to the media's efforts to portray a nation where African-Americans should be seen as innocent, noble, civilized victims of white oppression, more Rosa Parks than Nat Turner, a messianic slave who, inspired by an eclipse of the sun, led the mass-murder of fifty white people in 1831.

So "black rage" neither began nor ended with Mark Essex, but he became one of its most powerful symbols.

In 2002, snipers John Allen Muhammad and Boyd Lee Malvo killed sixteen people in a reign of terror as the "D.C. sniper," even plotting to kill white police officers in one grand finale. Muhammad was a twelve-year-old boy in Baton Rouge, Louisiana, on the day Mark Essex laid siege to the Howard Johnson, and it seems unlikely that he was not affected somehow by a case that drew stark divisions between white and black.

Nellie Essex buried her son's bullet-shredded body in Emporia six days after the shooting. There were no military honors. At his funeral, one memorial wreath bore a sash that said, "Power to the People."

The Black Panthers of New York sent a telegram to the family applauding Mark Essex as "a black man, warrior, and revolutionary."

For many years, Mark Essex's grave sat unmarked in Emporia's Maplewood Cemetery, not far from the grave of legendary newspaperman William Allen White. But his family eventually placed a modest granite stone, and local veterans now mark Essex's grave with a small bronze military medallion.

Among the many ironies and enigmas still surrounding the Howard Johnson massacre, there's this one: an

American flag is planted on Mark Essex's grave every Memorial Day.

TIM URSIN HAD NEVER HEARD OF MARK ESSEX, NEVER LOOKED HIM IN THE EYES. Their paths had never crossed until that miserable January morning at the Howard Johnson hotel.

While he heard fragments of the story as he drifted in and out of sedation at the hospital, he never heard the full story of what happened that day until about three weeks later. But by that time, he was involved in a different kind of fight.

During his six weeks in the hospital, Tim endured excruciating pain to save his arm.

As many as ten times, his wound was debrided, an agonizing procedure to strip away dead, rotting flesh from his wound. Doctors laid moist pig skin over the mutilated tissue to protect it from infection.

Later, surgeons planed paper-thin ribbons of skin from Tim's thigh to seal the wound permanently and to finally offer some relief from the electric ache of air hitting exposed meat and raw nerves.

But within his first two weeks, a repaired artery in his forearm burst. Rather than repair it, surgeons simply sealed it off, a risky move. A few weeks later, as a doctor examined his gangrenous thumb, he accidentally thrust his finger through the squishy rotten tissue of Tim's hand. So they removed the thumb in hopes of saving the rest of his left hand.

Things didn't get better. To stabilize the remaining palm and fingers, doctors inserted a stainless steel pin in the wrist-end of his shattered radius, but the pin eventually worked its way out through the skin of his hand.

His hand was now useless.

Tim had made many difficult decisions in his life, but the next one was easy. He asked his doctors to remove his mangled left hand entirely and replace it with a prosthetic stainless-steel hook.

While he was still in the hospital, the fire chief asked him to take on the department's public information job, but Tim wasn't a desk rider. If he couldn't fight fires, he didn't want to be around the firehouse where he'd be reminded more of his weaknesses than his strengths. If he couldn't ride a truck, he knew he would always be on the periphery of the brotherhood.

He leaned hard on his wife, Mary, in those dark days. A daughter and sister of firefighters, she never gave him a chance to feel sorry for himself. While he tried to keep himself together, she kept the family together. When people would stare at his hook, he felt more embarrassed for Mary and the kids than for himself.

When Tim's sick leave ended in 1975, he drifted. He worked as a concrete tester, a boat salesman, and a sporting goods clerk. He bought a boat and taught himself how to handle a fishing rod with his hook.

At first, friends were asking him to take them out on the bayous. Then he started doing a few weekend charters for rich fishermen from the interior.

By 1982, he was chartering fishing expeditions full time from Delacroix Island and now from Shell Beach, fishing the inland marshes and the outer bays for speckled trout and redfish. And he began to use a marketing slogan that, for better or worse, had literally come from above: Captain Hook.

When his fishermen ask, he often spins a wild tale about a hungry shark because it makes people laugh, but he makes no effort to hide the real story. Everybody on the water knows him as Captain Hook.

He still feels his phantom hand. He can tell you the exact position of it because when they clipped the tendons and tied them off, its sensory pose was fixed forever. The thumb is extended, the index and middle fingers spread apart, the ring finger curled in

And he keeps the brass nozzle that saved his life. It still bears the bullet hole that might have been in his neck if not for the simple intervention of a different unseen hand.

But he seldom imagines what he might say to Mark Essex if they were to meet, finally, face to face. It no longer matters. He wants only to live without the hate that consumed the man who tried to kill him for no better reason than the color of his skin.

Every morning, Tim Ursin, more than ever a devout Catholic, says a prayer and thanks God for another day. And at the end of every Saturday, he attends Mass without fail.

But he's philosophical about it. He bears no malice for Mark Essex, although he rarely speaks the name. He's lucky to be alive. And most importantly, he knows it.

"I've been living on borrowed time for more than thirty-five years," he says today. "It just wasn't my time."

In the evening after he voted, Tim was watching television when the phone rang.

It was the young black man he'd met at the election hall that morning.

"Look, I've been thinking about our conversation all day," the man said. "I came home and told my wife that I met you and that you told me your story and, well, I just kept thinking all day that you have a good way of looking at a bad thing."

"Thanks, man," Tim said. "I appreciate it."

"I'm sorry about the man   a black man   I don't feel that way   "

"Hey, this was one man," Tim said. "It wasn't personal and it doesn't make me feel any different about black people who don't think that way. You can't spend your life blaming others for what only a few bad people do. Hate will eat you up, man."

"Yeah, well, I guess you taught me some things, and I just wanted to say   "

The man paused for a long moment.

"I just wanted to say I won't ever forget you."

And for the first time in a long time, Tim cried.

Photo Archive II

Gravely wounded firefighter Tim Ursin received a commendation for the bravery he showed during Mark Essex's sniper rampage.

The hose nozzle that saved Ursin's life, bearing the bullet hole.

Tim Ursin revisits his old New Orleans fire station.

EVIL ON THE FRONT DOOR

The Baton Rouge Serial Killer, 2002

THE LANGUID BROWN WATER OF BAYOU TECHE RUNS AS SLOW AS A CEMETERY. It twists and turns among giant moss-bearded oaks, haunted swamps, and decaying mansions built with sugar money.

The meandering bayou's name comes from a local Indian word for "snake" because, in their culture's mythic history, a giant snake attacked their scattered villages, and it took many years for an army of warriors to kill it. The serpent's enormous corpse sunk into the Louisiana mud and rotted where it lay until the rain filled its death-hole with water.

Muddy Bayou Teche is the sclerotic artery through the heart of Cajun Country, where crawfish boils and Mass are both religious sacraments. On its shifting banks, Longfellow's Evangeline waited for her long-lost lover. And its syrupy water nourishes the very roots of Cajun history in the former French colony known as Louisiana.

Cecilia is one of the farming villages settled on the rich soil of Bayou Teche more than two hundred years ago. Today, it's one of those backwater places few people go unless they live there, but people are friendly enough to answer the door when somebody needs directions.

After all, people have been known to disappear into the *petite pluie fine*—the mists—of Bayou Teche.

GOSPEL MUSIC POURED FROM THE RADIO LIKE LIGHT. Dianne Alexander was humming along as she fixed lunch for her son Herman, who'd soon be home from his morning classes at the University of Louisiana in Lafayette, a half hour away.

She'd spent her morning running errands in Breaux Bridge and Lafayette, picking up groceries, gassing up, and stopping at the post office. A nursing student, she'd just started working the evening shift for her clinical studies at Lafayette General Medical Center, and she was grateful for a morning off. She only wished her husband Oliver, a delivery driver for a local seafood company, could be there to share that sultry July morning in 2002 with her, but he was off on a run to Houston and wouldn't be back until after she was at work later that night.

The errands took all morning, but Dianne's timing was perfect. She had time to make lunch and start dinner. She'd gotten home to the comfortable mobile home where she'd lived for twelve years, plopped her purse on the kitchen counter, and taken off her wedding ring, which she always did before cooking. While some turkey necks sizzled on the stove, she set up an ironing board in Herman's room so she could press her student nurse's uniform after lunch.

The daughter of a construction worker, Dianne was the second of seven children. Her strict father worked hard, but the family barely scraped by. She grew up with eight other people in a tiny, three-bedroom wood-frame bungalow in the black section of Breaux Bridge. They had a TV, but Dianne liked to listen to rhythm-and-blues shows on the radio while she helped her mama do the laundry on an old wringer machine on the back porch. She went to class in homemade clothes and played the xylophone in the school band.

Education wasn't a priority for her devoutly Catholic parents, but church was. Because Dianne was the family's only driver at age thirteen, this little girl who peered in the mirror and spoke to God quit school in the eleventh grade.

Dianne grew up tall and pretty. A light-skinned African-American woman with striking hazel eyes, she caught plenty of boys' attention, and she liked it. Although she'd met Oliver in high school, she was pregnant at eighteen by another boy. When that marriage fell apart, she and Oliver found each other again and eventually married.

She also found Jesus. Although faith ran through her like the beat in one of her beloved R&B songs, she had never been a staunch churchgoer until she picked up an evangelistic tract from a nearby church one day. *God knows the number of hairs on your head*, it said. The notion intrigued her. So she and a friend drove to the church one night and were caught up in a frenzy that excited her, made her feel good. She was saved that night.

Now at age forty-six, she lived with a hard-working man she loved in a house that sat on two acres of land in Cecilia, just up the road from where she grew up. Life hadn't always been easy, but she was a wife and a mother of four children, one going to college. She'd earned her GED years before and had been taking college classes since 1992 to become a nurse. She not only felt loved as she cooked and sang along to the gospel station, she felt safe.

Then came a knock on her door.

DIANNE OPENED THE DOOR TO FIND A BURLY YOUNG BLACK MAN STANDING ON HER COVERED PORCH.

He was tall and good-looking with a neatly trimmed mustache and light brown eyes. His hair was closely cut. Although he was slightly heavy, he was neatly dressed in a striped golf shirt, denim shorts, and sneakers with white ankle socks. He smiled as she opened the door.

"May I help you?"

"Hi, my name is Anthony," he said, shaking her hand. "I'm from Monroe. I'm supposed to be doing construction work for the Montgomerys. Do you know them?"

No, Dianne said, she didn't know of any Montgomery family in the area. But this man was well-spoken and pleasant, she thought, and she wanted to help if she could.

"Well do you think your husband would know them?"

"No, he wouldn't."

"Do you think I could use your phone? Maybe a phone book?" the young man said. "Maybe it'll have their address."

Dianne retrieved her cordless phone and directory from the kitchen and handed it to the man on her porch. While he flipped through the pages, she pushed her front door closed—leaving it open just a crack—and went back to the turkey necks boiling on the stove for Oliver's dinner, humming along with the radio. When the man started peeking through the thin gap of the door, she went back.

The man smiled at her.

"Oh, I ain't gonna do you anything," he said, smiling big. "But are you sure your husband doesn't know these Montgomerys?"

Dianne was adamant. "No, he doesn't know them."

He could hear the gospel music playing inside.

"I used to sing in a gospel choir," he said, stepping closer. "Maybe you've heard of us "

He gave Dianne a name she didn't recognize. She told him she hadn't heard of him, and she began to get a little annoyed at this chatty guy at her door. She had work to do.

"Are you sure you and your husband don't know the Montgomerys?" he asked again.

Dianne had heard enough from this annoying guy.

"Look, my husband isn't home," she said and started to close the front door.

The man suddenly plowed into the door to force his way inside. She tried to barricade the metal door but in the blink of an eye, his big hands were around Dianne's throat, and he shoved her against the door.

"Take me to your bedroom!" he demanded, as he pulled a blade out of his back pocket. "I have a knife! I'll stab you in the eye!"

Everything in Dianne wanted to scream out, to fight back, but she couldn't. Nothing seemed real. A stranger was in her home and she didn't know why, but she knew she couldn't lose her nerve. Instead, she tried to clear her head and speak as calmly as she could to her attacker, who gripped her windpipe. She didn't want to go to her small bedroom because there was only one way out.

"We don't have to go into the bedroom," she managed to whisper. "We can just stay right here."

With his hand still around her throat, the man walked her a few steps to the living room and eased her down onto the carpet.

"Take off your panties!" he told her.

"I can't. Your hand is on my throat," Dianne rasped, realizing exactly what was happening to her.

He removed his hand, and Dianne lifted her long denim skirt to slip off her panties. He spread her bare legs, propping one on the couch as he unzipped his shorts and played with himself. He touched her, trying to arouse himself. Bending down, he laid his freshly shaved cheek against hers.

"I'm just going to do this and then I'll leave," he said, almost tenderly.

"I'm not going to tell anybody."

Then he kissed her lips lightly and whispered in her ear.

"I've been watching you."

Sweaty and breathing harder now, he was trying to get an erection, but it wasn't happening. He even turned off the mobile home's humming air-conditioner so he could focus better.

Then he put the knife on the floor and tried to concentrate on his flaccid penis. Diane grabbed the knife, but the man took it away from her before she could use it.

"Where did you see me?" Dianne asked calmly. She was determined to be compliant, fearing he'd kill her if she fought back, resisted, or just made him mad. She studied everything about him—in case she survived. She wanted to be able to describe every detail.

"Shut up! Shut up!" he shouted. Still no erection.

"Can I turn off the fire on the stove?" Dianne asked matter-of-factly. She worried she might be killed and the house might burn down, destroying all the evidence.

"Fuck the pot!" he yelled.

He told her not to move while he took off his shirt and laid on top of her, sweating all over her, trying to get it up but unable to.

"Bitch!" he growled.

Frustrated, the man stood up and looked around the room. His eyes fell on a phone cord connecting the computer to a wall outlet. He cut a length of the cord with his knife.

"You're not a bad looking guy," she said, trying to stall.

"No, I'm not," he seethed.

He straddled Dianne's shoulders and lashed the cord around her neck, pulling it tight. Choking, she slipped a finger under the wire, but she couldn't fight back against the man's weight pinning her to the floor. Unable to penetrate her or strangle her, he flew into a rage, beating her with his fists and finally smashing a heavy ceramic pot on her head.

She passed out, bleeding profusely from a ragged gash in her forehead. Drifting in and out of consciousness, she'd sometimes awake to see him and feel him on top of her, still trying in vain to rape her but still unable to get an erection. She didn't know how long she lay there, half awake and half dead, while her attacker moved freely around her.

He was making one last effort to penetrate her when he suddenly looked up and listened intently. He had heard something he didn't expect: a car in the driveway.

Dianne watched him as he leapt up, dressed, and grabbed her purse and cordless phone. Frustrated at being interrupted—at losing control of the situation—he stomped Dianne hard in the stomach and fled out the back door just as her son Herman came in the front.

Dianne was numb and barely conscious. She felt no pain, just relief.

She was alive.

Herman had come home for lunch to find a strange car parked in his spot on the driveway. He noticed a gold-colored Mitsubishi Mirage that had front-end damage and a front license plate advertising a local dealer, Hampton Motors. It belonged to nobody he knew.

He went inside, and everything was quiet until he heard his mother's distressed voice in the living room.

"Help!" she cried. "Get a knife!"

Dianne was splayed on the bloody rug, her skirt pulled up around her waist and delirious. Her face was badly bruised, her eyes swollen shut. Then Herman saw the back door swinging open and ran outside to see the gold Mirage speeding away down Highway 31, with a silvery cord hanging from a rear window. He ran back inside, got his keys, and peeled out of the driveway to chase the man who attacked his mother, but he quickly lost sight of him.

When he returned to the mobile home, he followed a trail of blood to find his mother had stumbled into the bedroom, called 911, and passed out.

The next day, St. Martin's Parish cops released a composite sketch of Dianne's would-be rapist. What they didn't know at the time is that they were releasing the first public portrait of a serial killer.

WHEN DETECTIVES ARRIVED, THEY FOUND Herman waiting for them in the driveway, furious. His fury was so intense he couldn't describe what he'd seen.

Dianne was life-flighted to Lafayette General, where doctors found she had a skull fracture, many cuts and bruises around her neck, face, and scalp, and other injuries to the back of her head. They were unable to collect any of the attacker's DNA. Over the next five days in the hospital, while police scoured her home for clues, an investigator gently led her through the details and asked her to describe her assailant for a police sketch artist.

The next day, St. Martin's Parish cops released a composite sketch of Dianne's would-be rapist and a description of his gold Mitsubishi sedan.

What they didn't know at the time is that they were releasing the first public portrait of a serial killer. It never crossed their minds that this crime in little Cecilia could be related to a recent series of Baton Rouge killings.

And they didn't know that Dianne Alexander was his first and only living victim.

All the rest were dead. And there would be more.

THREE DAYS LATER, PAM KINAMORE, a forty-four-year-old mother and antique-store owner, disappeared from her Baton Rouge home one evening. Her nude, rotting corpse was found four days later under a swampland bridge 30 miles west of Baton Rouge, nearly decapitated by three vicious slashes across her throat. She had been raped.

The body, exposed to humid Louisiana summer heat and various bayou predators, was unidentifiable except for a gold wedding band on its left ring finger. It was Pam Kinamore's. But her husband noticed that the body was not wearing Pam's favorite thin silver toe ring.

Police also found a strand of phone cord near the body and collected it as evidence.

The medical examiner determined she'd been alive when her throat was cut because there was blood in her lungs.

Two witnesses reported seeing a white pickup truck driven by a white man with a naked, frightened, white female passenger matching Kinamore's description on the night she disappeared. Other than the DNA collected from her body, that was all the local cops had to go on.

White man. White pickup truck.

Within two weeks, police announced that trace DNA evidence conclusively linked the murder of Kinamore, a one-time beauty queen, to the same man who had killed at least two other local women in the past year: Gina Wilson Green, a forty-one-year-old nursing supervisor found strangled in September 2001; and Charlotte Murray Pace, a twenty-two-year-old grad student whose throat was slashed in a townhouse near the Louisiana State University campus the previous May.

News of a serial killer among them stunned the city of Baton Rouge, and a flood of questions were only starting to be asked—but not answered very well.

Like Kinamore, the two earlier victims were attractive white women with chestnut hair, and there had been no forced entry into any of their homes. But that's where the common characteristics ended.

Pace and Green both drove BMWs, but not Kinamore. Pace and Green both jogged on the same lakeside path near LSU, but not Kinamore. Green and Pace had lived a few doors from each other on the capital's Stanford Avenue, but Kinamore didn't live nearby. Green and Kinamore both loved antiques, but not Pace. Green and Kinamore were both older, petite women; Pace was tall and young.

LESS THAN A MONTH AFTER KINAMORE'S SLAYING, the Baton Rouge Multi-Agency Homicide Task Force was formed to find the serial killer, but it released precious little valuable information to the public, even though police agencies in the greater Baton Rouge area had more than sixty unsolved cases of missing or murdered women since 1985.

The task force lacked credibility almost from the start. The streets of the state capital were already alive with rumors, complicating the investigation. Scuttlebutt pegged the killer as a professor at LSU, a BMW salesman, or a cop. It said he played tapes of crying babies outside so women would open their doors. The police themselves fueled the hysteria by telling the frightened citizens of Baton Rouge the killer was a white man driving a white pickup.

Pride played a role, too. When criminologist Robert Keppel, who helped investigate the crimes of Ted Bundy and the Green River Killer, offered to help the Baton Rouge task force, it declined.

Women swarmed to self-defense classes and started

carrying guns. Every white guy in a white pickup got suspicious looks from passing motorists and pedestrians.

Task force members wanted to bet on statistics. They put their faith in the tendencies of serial killers to use the same methods, stalk identical kinds of victims, and avoid crossing racial borders.

So the task force also dismissed other possibly related cases brought to them by other cops. The January stabbing of white, brunette Geralyn De Soto in West Baton Rouge was ignored because she had not been raped, her wounds were not as vicious, and the murder happened in West Baton Rouge, a decidedly different jurisdiction. Besides, her husband was the prime suspect.

Nobody had yet studied the DNA of human tissue found beneath Geralyn's fingernails, or they would have known that she, too, was killed by the same man.

FBI profiler May Ellen O'Toole built a portrait of the killer. She said he was likely between twenty-five and thirty-five. He was big and strong, weighing up to one hundred seventy-five pounds. His shoe size was between ten and eleven. He earned an average wage or less, money was tight, and he probably didn't deal with the public in his job.

He blends into the community and is seen as harmless. When he loses control of a situation, he regresses to primitive anger. And he blames other people when he loses control.

He hadn't expected Pam Kinamore's body to be found, O'Toole surmised, so he might have gone back to the crime scene to see where he screwed up.

Going deeper into his psychology, O'Toole said the killer stalked his victims, who were likely to be attractive women of a higher social class. He might even have chatted with them before his attacks. He wanted to be appealing, but he was too unsophisticated to truly relate to them.

He likely gave odd, unexpected gifts to the women in his life, possibly even "trophies" he'd taken from victims. He didn't handle rejection well but was cool under pressure. Because he chose high-risk targets at high-risk times of day, he liked the excitement of the attack. Despite his planning, he was impulsive. In relationships, he was hot-tempered and irritable. He was, like most serial killers, without remorse or empathy. Worse, the killer was learning from his mistakes and evolving. And as time wore on, he was likely to become increasingly paranoid.

She didn't say whether he was white or black, but whether they'd watched too many TV crime shows or their suspicions had been influenced by witnesses who swore they saw a white man in a white truck, police were focused only on white men. For them, it was a safe bet because fewer than one in six American serial killers are black.

But profiles don't catch killers. Cops do. And in this case, Baton Rouge authorities were making a series of crucial errors, dismissing leads and looking the wrong way. More than fifteen hundred white men were swabbed for DNA samples. The task force bought a billboard in the interstate with a sketch of their suspected killer—a white man. Cops announced what kinds of shoes the killer wore at two murder scenes, causing some veteran investigators to worry he'd destroy the evidence.

Worse, police began to realize they might have more than one serial killer prowling Baton Rouge at the same time, a frightening if mathematically unlikely possibility.

Mounting public hysteria was confusing matters even more. More than 27,000 tips flooded in from the public and swamped the task force. Many leads were simply ignored, even when they came from other police agencies. When Dianne Alexander's composite sketch was shared with Baton Rouge cops, they dismissed it because her would-be rapist was black and drove a Mitsubishi. Their killer was a white man driving a white pickup. Moreover, Dianne was black—although very fair—and their killer favored white women.

On September 4, a woman called the task force to tell them that she knew the killer, a man named Derrick Todd Lee, her convicted stalker. But when investigators went to Lee's house and saw he was a pudgy black man and didn't drive a white work truck, they dismissed him as a suspect.

Enter Detective David McDavid, a small-town cop from Zachary, 15 miles north of Baton Rouge. In 1992, he'd worked the disappearance and murder of Connie Warner, a forty-one-year-old mother abducted from her Zachary home with no signs of forced entry. Her badly decomposed body was found in a Baton Rouge ditch eleven days later.

A year later, he caught the case of two necking teenagers who were slashed by a machete-wielding peeping Tom in a cemetery. The attacker ran away when a cop drove up to roust the kids. One of the victims later identified a local troublemaker well-known to Zachary cops: Derrick Todd Lee, a petty burglar, stalker, and peeper with a long rap sheet.

Then in 1998, Detective McDavid pulled another missing-persons case. Twenty-eight-year-old single mom Randi Mebruer had disappeared from her Zachary home. A pool of blood congealed on the floor and her three-year-old son wandered in the front yard, but her body was never found. McDavid quickly noticed that Mebruer lived just around the corner from the house where Connie Warner had disappeared six years before—and in a neighborhood where Derrick Todd Lee was suspected of peeping for the past year or so.

Armed with the evidence in those three cases, McDavid went to the Baton Rouge task force. And the task force sent him away.

Meanwhile, women were disappearing and dying.

On Thanksgiving Day 2002, twenty-three-year-old Marine recruit Trineisha Dene Colomb was visiting her dead mother's grave in Grand Coteau, Louisiana, when she vanished. Her car was found near the grave, and a hunter later found her body along a path in a wooded area in the Lafayette suburb of Scott. She'd been savagely beaten and raped, her head slammed against a tree trunk, and her dead body left to be eaten by vermin.

The task force didn't think Colomb's murder was related. It didn't happen in her home. Colomb was half-black. She wasn't stabbed.

But a key piece of evidence was left behind: DNA. Two days before Christmas 2002, the state crime lab confirmed that Trineisha Dene Colomb had been killed by the man they now called the South Louisiana Serial Killer, but his identity was no clearer.

On Christmas Eve, Mari Ann Fowler disappeared from the sidewalk in front of a Subway restaurant in Port Allen, just across the Mississippi River from Baton Rouge. Her body was never found.

And on March 3, 2003, Carrie Lynn Yoder, a twenty-six-year-old doctoral student at LSU, disappeared from her Baton Rouge apartment. Ten days later, a fisherman found her beaten body floating half-naked in the water near the Whisky Bay Bridge, where Pam Kinamore's body had been discovered eight months before. Her killer had beaten her so severely that nine ribs had been snapped from her spinal column, puncturing her liver and lungs. Her face was so badly damaged that she had to be identified by dental records.

DNA evidence showed her to be the fifth official victim of the Baton Rouge serial killer.

The task force was stunned by what came next: sophisticated tests of the killer's DNA showed he was a black man. Specifically, scientists told the task force, his genetic makeup was eighty-five percent Sub-Saharan African and fifteen percent Native American.

Everything they thought they knew was crap.

AROUND THE SAME TIME, FORMER NEIGHBORS OF CONNIE WARNER and Randi Mebruer in Zachary started to report that their long-time peeping Tom was back, and police found evidence that it was true.

That's when a veteran detective named Dannie Mixon began to look deeper into Derrick Todd Lee, a serial peeper who was now thirty-four years old and long a suspect in the Zachary crimes. He knew about Todd's abusive father and domineering mother. He knew Todd was learning disabled and had spent time in special classes, where he sucked his thumb and called the teacher "mama." He knew how Todd had tortured his dog and puppies as a kid. He knew Todd learned early in life how to talk his way out of trouble and cast blame on others.

He knew every car Lee had ever driven. He knew Lee's good days and bad days—and he saw that the killings often happened just after Lee lost a job, or money was low, or he got thumped by his probation officer. And he noticed that Lee, who had been in and out of jail on a variety of raps, was always out of jail when the five known victims were killed—and when Connie Warner and Randi Mebruer died or disappeared.

Armed with the added evidence that the Baton Rouge serial killer was an African-American, Mixon convinced a judge to issue a search warrant to swab Lee for DNA.

On May 5, Dannie Mixon went to Lee's home and took the swab himself, but he didn't need science to tell him what his gut had already told him. They had the right guy.

The next day, while police waited for the results of his DNA test, Derrick Todd Lee told his wife something was about "to blow up on us" and that police would try to pin a crime on him. He quickly packed a bag and took a bus to Chicago but, oddly, he returned three days later. In another frantic rush, he and his wife abruptly pulled their two children out of school, cleaned out their little brick house in the small town of Starhill, north of Baton Rouge, giving some possessions to friends and family, and throwing others—like their sofa—in a dumpster behind a truck stop. They spent their last night in a motel before saying a final goodbye as Lee sent his family to Detroit.

Then he boarded another bus to Atlanta. There, he moved into a cheap motel, got a job on a construction crew, and used his first paycheck to pay for a barbecue for his new buddies. He didn't have a car, so he bummed rides to local pawn shops where he hocked gold jewelry. He didn't waste time finding companionship: the smooth-talking Lee dated several women in Atlanta and promised them cognac if they would come to his room. Despite his flirtations, Lee even started a Bible study group among the motel's fifty or so tenants.

But on May 25, a Sunday, the Louisiana crime lab delivered the shocking news that Derrick Todd Lee was the Baton Rouge serial killer. His DNA matched trace evidence found on the five dead women.

Police rushed to his house and battered down the door, but found the home abandoned. Neighbors said he'd skipped town two weeks before. Cops had no idea where he or his family had gone. A serial killer was in the wind.

The task force named their killer in a press conference and distributed Lee's picture. The *Baton Rouge Advocate* trumpeted WANTED in war-type over a front-page blow-up of an old mug shot of Derrick Todd Lee, and the local TV station went wall-to-wall with coverage.

The news seeped all the way to Detroit, where Lee's wife was staying with her aunt and uncle. That night, her family called the FBI.

Lee's wife said he was in Atlanta, but she didn't know where. She said she knew nothing about any murders.

Back in Louisiana, cops were interrogating one of Lee's mistresses when her phone rang. It was him. Caller ID showed a number in the 404 area code—Atlanta. When cops called it back, a Pakistani motel manager answered. He confirmed Lee was staying at the motel in a $135-a-week efficiency.

The next morning, police, marshals, and FBI agents descended on the dowdy Lakewood Motor Lodge in Atlanta, but Lee had already checked out. They scoured the city without luck until, late on the night of May 26, an Atlanta patrol officer found a man resembling Lee wandering around a tire store in southwest Atlanta.

"Can I see some identification?" the cop asked.

The man calmly handed over his driver's license and without so much as an unkind word, Derrick Todd Lee—possibly the worst serial killer in Louisiana's often bloody history—was arrested three days after his own DNA betrayed him.

All the clues were soon to fall into place: the phone cord from Dianne Alexander's home found near Pam Kinamore's body, souvenirs taken from dead women, stolen phones, the shoe bloody prints found at crime scenes, the vehicles, the timeline   it would all come together like a million-piece puzzle.

Back at the police station, Lee had very little to say.

"Y'all might as well go ahead and give me the needle," he told his interrogators before he stopped talking altogether. "I'm closing the book."

He said nothing as he was booked for the murder of Carrie Yoder and the attempted rape of Dianne Alexander, fingerprinted, and locked up. He waived extradition and the next morning was flown home to Louisiana on an FBI jet to face his accusers.

And the star witness against him, besides his own DNA, would be the only woman who'd survived an attack by Derrick Todd Lee.

Dianne Alexander.

DERRICK TODD LEE STAYED TRUE TO HIS PROMISE TO CLOSE THE BOOK ON HIS CRIMES. He never spoke about any of them.

During police interrogations immediately after his arrest, he insisted repeatedly, "I got no story to tell." He told them he didn't understand DNA, said he'd made peace with God, and didn't care whether he was executed, even flirted subtly with FBI profiler Mary Ellen O'Toole. And he had plenty to say about police harassment and all the women who looked down on him.

"I'm here to tell you I done walked around man, with, uh, a lot on my mind, a lot in my heart, bro, a lot of sleepless nights because there was some things I got accused of I know I ain't had nothin' to do with it," he said.

"I done been in the wrong place at the wrong time, you know, dealin' with women. I been dealing with women or done slept with some women you, uh, you're probably sayin' I'm gonna tell you a lie about. I can bring some women name up, you know, right now, and you probably go and ask them. Say, 'You ever been with Derrick?' They'll tell you no. But I know and that person know, you know what I'm sayin'?

"I been with women where I didn't want to get seen, be seen with me in a date, but like, you know what I'm sayin', I done been there. I remember women, like they high society, and then when they was around they friends, they didn't want they friends to know they was dealin'. You know, everybody got they little skeletons in they closet

"I done been with some women, where some women tell me, say, 'Lord, if somebody see you here, they'll ask me what's wrong with me.' I done been through all that in my life."

But that was the closest Derrick Todd Lee ever came to explaining his crimes, with vague references to oversexed "high society" women who were too pretentious to be seen with him, and the torture it caused.

He had nothing to say about the dead women, nor the missing women linked to him, nor any victims whose names were still not known. He refused to offer anything that looked like a confession, except to say that it didn't bother him in the least if they "electrocuted me up" because he was right with God, and that's all that mattered.

On August 5, 2004, in Port Allen, Derrick Todd Lee stood before a jury of six men and six women to answer for the second-degree murder of Geralyn De Soto, the first of many trials he was to face. In this case, he faced a maximum of life in prison because prosecutors lacked the necessary aggravating elements for a death sentence—and still had better cases ahead.

DeSoto, only twenty-one, was found stabbed and beaten to death in her home in the small town of Addis, across the river from Baton Rouge, on the same day she registered for graduate school at LSU in January 2002. Evidence suggested that just before noon that day, someone broke into her mobile home, bludgeoned her with a telephone, and stabbed her three times. Still alive, she ran to her bedroom, where she grabbed a shotgun, but her attacker snatched it from her before cutting her throat from ear to ear—so deep that it scraped across her spinal column—and sadistically stomping her belly. He did not rape her.

Bloody boot prints matching Lee's shoes were found, and the knife he used to slice De Soto's throat was found in his vehicle.

In her fight, De Soto herself had collected the evidence that would eventually identify her attacker. It was beneath her fingernails. Ultimately, science proved it matched only four-tenths of one percent of all the males on Earth—and one of them was Derrick Todd Lee. Even more damning, Lee's DNA contained rare markers that raised the odds that somebody else killed Geralyn De Soto to thirty trillion-to-one.

If modern science had built a solid case against Derrick Todd Lee, prosecutors were counting on Dianne Alexander to put a human face on his atrocities. As his only known survivor, she would bear witness to Lee's murderous methods.

Tense and frightened, she came into the courtroom, swore to tell the truth, and sat facing Derrick Todd Lee for the first time since her attack two years before. But she didn't look at him. She didn't have to.

She answered questions clearly and without flourish as she recounted the summer day Derrick Todd Lee stood on her doorstep, appealing to her kindness as a way to get what he wanted. She told the jury how he had threatened to stab her in the eye, made her take off her panties, tried unsuccessfully to get an erection, choked her with the phone cord, beat her savagely, and then fled in frustration when her son arrived home.

"I have no idea how many times he hit me," she testified. "I only remember the first blow."

Asked if she saw the man who attacked her, Dianne pointed directly at Lee, who sat emotionless at the defense table, and seemed to speak directly to him.

"While my eyes were closed, I did not forget your face."

The defense asked her about the police sketch and the make of car her son had seen, arguing that Lee was not the man she described. But the cross-examination was brief.

As Dianne stepped off the witness stand, the prosecutor scanned the faces of jurors. They had been touched by her story. They liked her.

The next day, Lee interrupted the proceedings to ask the judge whether he could fire his court-appointed lawyer, whom he believed was not being aggressive enough.

"My life is on the line here," he argued at the bench. "He ain't representing me like he said.   He lied to me from go, from day one."

But the judge told him he couldn't fire a public defender and that his only other choice was to represent himself. Lee relented and the trial continued as evidence against him mounted. The primary defense was simple: the prosecution hadn't connected all the dots, they were exploiting the public's misdirected and white-hot anger, and DNA was unreliable.

After four days of testimony, the jury required just one hour and forty minutes to find Derrick Todd Lee guilty of second-degree murder in the death of Geralyn DeSoto. Six days later, the judge sentenced Lee to life in Louisiana State Penitentiary at Angola, without the possibility of parole.

As the prison van drove away, Lee banged his head against the inside wall.

But his trials, literally and figuratively, were not finished.

Two months after his conviction in Geralyn De Soto's killing, Lee faced a new trial for the murder of Charlotte Murray Pace, a twenty-two-year-old student slain just two months before the attack on Dianne Alexander, who would again be the star human witness against Lee.

This time, Lee (with a new court-appointed defense team) faced the death penalty.

Of all the cases linked to Lee, Pace's had the grisliest crime scene. She had been raped and then she had been stabbed eighty-three times with a knife and a twelve-inch flat-blade screwdriver. One of the thrusts had gone through her eye into her brain. Her throat was cut, her skull fractured with a clothes iron, her face mutilated, and her hands terribly bruised, as though she'd fought her attacker to the death. Bloodstains were smeared and splattered throughout her townhouse, suggesting she'd struggled from room to room, even though she was gravely wounded. The killer had taken "trophies": a Louis Vuitton wallet containing a BMW key, a silver ring, her driver's license, and a cell phone.

This time, the judge allowed prosecutors to also introduce evidence in the murders of Pam Kinamore, Carrie Yoder, Trineisha Dene Colomb, and Gina Wilson Green—all connected by Derrick Todd Lee's DNA—as evidence of his methods and psychopathy.

And once again, DNA evidence was insurmountable. A forensic scientist testified that the unique markers in Lee's DNA were so rare that the probability of anyone else having the same genetic code was one-in-3.6 quadrillion—or 500,000 times the Earth's current population.

A steady stream of witnesses told the grisly story of five women's horrific killings, describing the last time they saw their friends and loved ones alive, and pointing to grisly crime scene photos while a subdued Lee sat and listened quietly.

THE LAST WITNESS TO TAKE THE STAND WAS DIANNE ALEXANDER. Inside she was nervous, but outwardly she was poised.

Again, she calmly recounted the sequence of the attack in vivid and succinct detail. She told how Lee had threatened to stab her in the eye—as Pace had been. She told how he had cut the phone cord to strangle her—the same cord fragment found near the body of Pam Kinamore. And how the bare-chested Lee had sweated on her during his frustrated rape attempt—sweat found on the collar of her dress that matched Lee's DNA.

Again, she relived the horror visited upon her.

Again, she was called to point to her attacker, sitting just a few feet away, watching her.

"Are you sure?" the prosecutor asked her.

"Positive. Without a shadow of a doubt. I'll never forget that face."

The desperate defense called her a liar. They said her testimony had changed over time. They said she was coached by prosecutors. They said she described a different man to the police artist. But Dianne held firm, and the jury was visibly angry at the hostile questioning.

The prosecution rested after that and, to everyone's surprise, so did the defense.

During closing arguments, some jurors wept openly as the prosecutor showed the smiling portraits of the dead women and begged them to find Lee guilty; the defense again railed against the fallibility of DNA testing and listed a dozen inconsistencies and holes in the prosecution's case. But the jury of six men and six women took only eighty minutes to find Lee guilty of Charlotte Murray Pace's first-degree murder.

During the penalty phase, Lee's lawyers argued that he was mentally retarded and thus, under a recently U.S. Supreme Court ruling, could not be executed. Expert witnesses on both sides disagreed about Lee's mental capacities.

This time, the same jury took ninety-three minutes to delivered Derrick Todd Lee's sentence: death.

Afterward, they said it was the strength of the DNA evidence and Dianne Alexander's testimony that convinced them of Lee's guilt.

Today, Lee sits in Angola's Death Row, monitored twenty-four hours a day. He spends all but one hour a day in his cell.

In 2008, the Louisiana Supreme Court upheld his death sentence. A tangle of appeals is ongoing, and no execution date has been set.

Charges in Lee's other alleged murders were dropped once he was sentenced to die. The charges Lee faced in Dianne Alexander's 2002 attack were set aside after she told prosecutors she wanted "to end a difficult period of her life and move on."

To date, Derrick Todd Lee has been officially linked by his distinctive DNA to seven murders, and he is strongly believed to have committed four others. A dozen more South Louisiana slayings over the twenty years before his arrest bear frightening similarities to his known crimes, but they might never be solved.

EVERY DAY SINCE DERRICK TODD LEE INVADED HER HOME AND HER LIFE, every morning for Dianne Alexander has been a little like waking up and starting life over.

And not necessarily in a bad way.

She graduated from nursing school with honors. She is writing a book about her experience as Lee's sole survivor. She dreams of taking up painting. And she has fallen in love all over again with her husband Oliver.

Not that life has been easy. The trauma churned up her whole family. Dianne's husband and son cleaned up her blood themselves. For months, Oliver spent his free moments driving around Lafayette and Baton Rouge looking in vain for that gold Mitsubishi Mirage. If he found it   well, he didn't know what he would do.

For a while, Dianne's hate for Lee was a wriggling maggot deep down inside, small but ultimately destructive. She couldn't go back to the house where she had once felt so comfortable, so safe, so she and Oliver lived with relatives until they could sell the place and get another.

Dianne's post-traumatic stress was real. She drifted through periods of volatile anger and eviscerating depression. She would scream and lash out at those closest to her, who were also suffering in the turbulent wake of Derrick Todd Lee. Arguments always circled back around, sometimes viciously, to the attack.

Because their eyewitness testimony and evidence had

been critical to the capture of Derrick Todd Lee, Dianne and son Herman eventually sought $150,000 in reward money offered by Crime Stoppers of Baton Rouge and Lafayette, but they were refused. The organization said its policies prevented it from rewarding crime victims, even if they were the keys to arresting a serial killer. A 2006 lawsuit by the Alexanders against Crime Stoppers is still wending through the courts.

She still doesn't know why Derrick Todd Lee chose her. Maybe her creamy, coffee-colored skin and hazel eyes made her look white from a distance. Maybe she lived in a place where nobody would hear her scream. Or maybe she was simply the first person he saw when his compulsion kicked in. Nobody knows because Derrick Todd Lee has never spoken about any of the cases.

Dianne believes fervently that his inability to rape her was because of her compliance. He lusted for a struggle. But she didn't give it to him. Her submission to his attack, at least in her mind, neutralized his sado-sexual compulsion. But, again, nobody knows.

Eventually, Dianne and Oliver sought counseling, and for Dianne especially, the church was a comfort. A couple times a week, she faithfully attends an evangelical church in a Lafayette strip mall, not far from where she now lives with Oliver in a small town west of the city, and she can hardly speak of the attack without invoking God in some way.

"Let God deal with him," she says today.

That's why she no longer hates Lee. She takes God's word about forgiveness. A death-penalty opponent, she certainly doesn't await his pending execution with any particular eagerness. If anything, she says, she'll pray for his soul.

"I gotta let it go," she says now, "because if I don't, it'll destroy me before it destroys him."

Photo Archive III

Dianne and Oliver Alexander, around the time of the 2002 attack.

Today, lone survivor Dianne Alexander has found peace in her faith.

Derrick Todd Lee after his 2003 arrest.

A FLOOD OF EVIDENCE

Ada Leboeuf

AFTER HER LOVER KILLED HER HUSBAND in an alligator-infested bayou, the townspeople of Morgan City, Louisiana began to call Ada Leboeuf "the Siren of the Swamps" and "Louisiana's Love Pirate." To her face she remained the more genteel Miss Ada – until she was hanged.

Ada Bonner was born in Morgan City, described as *"conveniently located right in the middle of everywhere"* because it is – New Orleans is an hour east, Baton Rouge the same distance north, and Lafayette is west. The town sits on the banks of the Atchafalaya River and is famous for the ocean-going vessels traveling its ship canal and for its hybrid blackberries, history of hurricanes, sugar mills, and the Union Army's Fort Starr.

The Roaring Twenties may have loosened America's morals with jazz and bathtub gin, but nothing was more important in Morgan City in 1927 than being "respectable." The Bonner family was respectable. Miss Ada's husband, James Leboeuf (often misspelled LeBouef) was respectable. The town doctor, Thomas Dreher, was respectable. That all changed on July 1, 1927 when Ada, Dreher, and a hit man murdered her husband.

Just four months earlier, Ruth Snyder, a Queens, New York housewife and mother, staged her husband's murder to look like a burglary gone wrong. She had the help of her lover, Henry Judd Gray. She had persuaded her husband to buy some extra life insurance. In the film based on the case, *Double Indemnity*, Gray is depicted as the life insurance salesman who wrote the policy that paid double in the event of an accidental death. In truth, Gray was a corset salesman. The case was sordid and sexy and not at all respectable, and fascinated the country.

When Louisiana had its own love and murder triangle at nearly the same time, newspapers, including The *New York Times*, ate up every word written about the lovers, the murder, their trial, and their comeuppance.

As one writer said of Snyder and Gray, after murder, their second greatest crime was simply being stupid. The same can be said for Ada Leboeuf and Thomas Dreher.

At the time of the murder, Ada Leboeuf was thirty-seven years old, and a pretty, middle-class housewife and mother of four. Her husband of twenty years was the superintendent of the local power plant, which delivered electricity to the town of about six thousand people and had subsidiaries across the state.

At best, Ada was an inattentive mother to her four children. It was said of her that she "[bore] the cares of motherhood lightly." She wasn't the town's best cook and her house usually needed a good cleaning. The nicest compliment neighbors could pay her was that her three sons and daughter were always nicely dressed.

Although well-thought of, people knew that James Leboeuf had a temper and that his marriage to Ada had its ups and downs.

Dr. Thomas Dreher, the local doctor, was well-liked, too. Both James Leboeuf and Dr. Dreher, who was in his late forties to mid-fifties, and married with three children, were active in civic affairs and became friends. Apparently, their wives did not, even before the scandal.

Leboeuf traveled often on business, and Ada had a tendency to get bored. When she got bored, she suffered from headaches and Dreher would make a house call. The people of Morgan City admitted he had a great bedside manner, but questioned why Miss Ada's headaches occurred only when her husband was out of town. Then word got around that he and Miss Ada were also meeting at a "Negro cabin" for privacy.

There couldn't be much about Miss Ada the doctor didn't know – he had, after all, delivered her four children. But there must have been some mystery or magic because he risked his marriage and respectability.

Miss Ada and the doctor had a code. If James was at home, she would hang a pillow case in the window, as if it had been washed and was drying. No pillow case meant that James was away and the coast was clear for a rendezvous. It didn't fool the neighbors.

Two years after the doctor and Miss Ada began their affair, a story spread that Dreher and Ada were seen swimming naked together in the bayou. And, someone wrote anonymous letters to Dr. Dreher's wife.

One read:

> *Two nights ago there was a lady and a man in that empty shack in the bayou. One of them was Ada Leboeuf and the other was your husband!*

Mrs. Dreher showed the note to James Leboeuf and he confronted Ada. He accused of her of having an affair and bloodied her nose at least once. His anger and jealousy took a strange turn when he dressed in his wife's clothes and drove around Morgan City with a loaded shotgun on the passenger seat – hoping Dr. Dreher would mistake him for Ada and flag him down. Then he planned to empty the shotgun into his rival.

At the same time, Miss Ada convinced Dreher that he was in danger. The two of them began to devise a scheme to get rid of her suspicious husband.

IN THE 1920S, MORGAN CITY WAS POPULATED by the upper echelon like Leboeuf and Dreher, and by another species – the men who made their living as frog catchers, trappers, moonshiners and alligator hunters. They did their hunting from pirogues, a type of canoe, and often caught their prey with their bare hands.

James Beadle was one of them. He was in his forties, and was a trapper and handyman.

On July 1, 1927 Miss Ada sent a note to Dr. Dreher.

> *Jim and me will go boat riding tonight on the lake. I talked to him and I believe he will treat you friendly, so meet us tonight and fix this up friendly and we will be friends. I am tired of living this way hearing Jim say he is going to kill both of us.*
>
> *As ever, Ada.*

Truth was, her motivation was more about murder than making peace.

Ada cozied up to her husband and suggested a moonlight boat trip, like the old days.

That evening, sometime after sunset, Dreher and Beadle took a boat out onto Lake Palourde. Ada and James Leboeuf went out in two boats, as was their custom.

She went home alone.

For several days Ada went about her business, taking care of the house and her four children. She told neighbors that she and James had had an argument and he had left.

She seemed unconcerned and never reported her husband's disappearance to the police.

The body of James Leboeuf might never have been found if it wasn't for the Great Mississippi River Flood of 1927. It began with heavy rains the year before, which caused the Mississippi River to bust its levees leaving 27,000 square miles under water. It killed hundreds of people and left hundreds of thousands homeless.

But the worst of the rains and flooding were over by the summer of 1927. One minute the rivers and bayous near Morgan City were so deep it seemed anything thrown in was gone forever, and the next minute the flood waters suddenly receded.

That's when Miss Ada's bad luck began. Late in the evening of July 6, 1927, just five days after she was sure she'd seen the last of her husband, fishermen hunting for frogs to sell to upscale restaurants hit James Leboeuf's body with their boat. The man had been shot twice, then gutted, slit from throat to belly, apparently to help the body sink. Heavy irons were tired around his neck and ankles. Much of his face had been eaten by crabs, but there was enough left to identify him.

Just a few hours after Leboeuf's body was found, Ada was brought in for questioning. She confessed to taking her husband out in the boat, but said that rather than reconcile with his friend, the doctor, her husband raised the gun he had brought along. "Friends be damned!" Leboeuf had yelled as he aimed and shot at Dreher. Ada said it was Beadle, the handyman, who then shot her husband. When James fell, she turned and rowed for shore. Eventually she told three versions of what happened.

Dreher was arrested at his home and claimed Beadle had shot Leboeuf – but his story varied in an important way from Ada's. Dreher said she waited and watched as the two men, in their panic, mutilated her husband's body and weighed it down so it would sink. And, Ada's longtime lover said *she* had initiated the murder, asking him to get rid of her husband.

At first, Beadle denied being present. He later insisted Dreher had fired the fatal shots and then used his surgical skills to make the incision in Leboeuf's abdomen. Beadle said they considered taking the body to the police and explaining it was self-defense, but in their panic they hoped to make the body disappear. Everyone agreed Leboeuf had fired first.

Just three weeks after LeBoeuf's body was found, Ada, Dreher and Beadle stood trial. It was a national sensation. Hundreds of people crowded the courtroom every day to hear the juicy evidence. Love letters were read aloud and the spectators learned that Ada may have tried to poison her husband two years before.

Ada was photographed wearing a smart knee-length dress, a broad-brimmed hat, and heels on her way to court. During her incarceration she was permitted unlimited visitations and her favorite rocking chair from home was brought to her cell.

Beadle wisely asked to have separate legal representation and had pro-bono attorneys. Dreher mortgaged his home and paid the legal fees for Ada and himself.

It was reported that the doctor spent the time waiting for the jury's verdict mopping his brow furiously, while the black widow watched the clock and the trapper chewed his tobacco.

On August 6, 1927 the jury returned unanimous guilty verdicts and recommended leniency for James Beadle. (He was sentenced to life and was released after serving ten years in prison.)

There was no leniency for Miss Ada and Dr. Dreher. They stood and heard the judge pronounce their sentence:

"You, Ada Bonner Leboeuf and you T. E. Dreher, are to be hanged by the neck until you are dead."

Following the trial, attorneys worked to get a reprieve for both. Despite how far Miss Ada and Dr. Dreher had fallen, fickle public opinion was on their side. Even the jurors who had handed down the convictions signed a petition requesting leniency. There were a couple of temporary reprieves, one just four hours before the scheduled hanging. In the end, the lovers waited for Governor Huey P. Long to grant them clemency, but he didn't.

RUTH SNYDER AND HENRY JUDD GRAY were executed at Sing Sing, one right after the other, on January 12, 1928. A reporter secretly photographed Snyder at the moment electricity ran through her body.

Just over a year later, on February 1, 1929, Ada Leboeuf and Thomas Dreher were hanged. The night before, Dreher wrote a letter for a nephew to give to the Associated Press. It was published in the *New York Times* and in other papers across the country that had reported every sordid detail of the affair. In the letter he said he was innocent, and that he and Miss Ada had tried to stop Beadle from killing James Leboeuf:

> *Poor Mrs. Leboeuf and I go to our doom tomorrow, two innocent souls.*
>
> *Neither Mrs. Leboeuf nor I fear death. We do not fear death because we have made our peace with God and we will soon be where*

> *suffering and punishment are no more, safe at home with Jesus. Thousands know, as well as Mrs. Leboeuf and I know, that we are innocent.*
>
> *Beadle killed Leboeuf and mutilated and disposed of his body over my protest and against my wishes, saying he had done the same thing to a man years ago and nothing ever came of it.*
>
> *All this story that Mrs. Leboeuf and I were lovers is untrue. I had been the Leboeuf's family physician for twenty years and Jim Leboeuf was my best friend until that lying anonymous letter came to light. I had always prized the friendship of the Leboeufs.*
>
> *A kinder hearted or more sympathetic woman never lived than Mrs. Leboeuf.* One wonders how his wife, the mother of his three children, felt when she read that.

One version of their last day was that, allowed to see each other one last time, they held hands and sobbed together before they were hanged. "Ada, don't get nervous; brace up," he told her.

"All right, doctor," she answered.

His parting words to her were, "Goodbye, I hope we will meet in the other world."

Another version is that Ada refused to see Dreher prior to the execution, explaining matter-of-factly, "He's not my family doctor anymore."

Miss Ada wore a pink housedress and the jailer tied her skirt around her knees so it would not balloon immodestly like a parachute when she fell to her death.

Ada was hung first. The first woman to be executed in

Louisiana, she is said to have pleaded: "Don't let me hang there too long. Don't make me suffer any more than I have to. Oh God. Isn't this a terrible thing? Oh God, who can do this thing? It is worse than murder itself."

The doctor was calmer and spoke to a reporter in the room. "Mr. Frost, you know we didn't do it." When the rope was around his neck he said his last words: "Oh, God, have mercy. Just don't let me choke to death."

The newspapers reported that both died instantly. After her death, her body was taken to the home of her brother. "There is an innocent girl," her elderly mother said as friends passed by the casket.

The body of Dr. Dreher was buried in his hometown of Clinton. His wife and two daughters attended the funeral.

On the same day, in a drenching rain, a small group of people followed Ada's body to the cemetery in Morgan City. She was buried beside the body of her husband, slain nineteen months earlier while out for a ride on a river in the moonlight.

Photo Archive IV

Ada Bonner LeBoeuf juggled marriage, four children and an affair with the town doctor.

Smartly dressed, Ada LeBoeuf is escorted to trial.

Dr. Thomas Dreher was a respected member of the town of Morgan City, LA and a good friend of his lover's husband.

Coming just months after the sensational trial of Ruth Snyder and Judd Gray in New York, the trial was front page news across the country.

BLACK WIDOW IN A PURE WHITE DRESS

Stephanie Cook

Copyright 2015 by Gregg Olsen and Rebecca Morris
Edited by Rebecca Morris
All Rights Reserved
Book Cover Design by BEAUTeBOOK
No part of this publication may be reproduced, stored in a retrieval system, or transmitted, in any form or by any means, electronic, mechanical, photocopying, recording, or otherwise, without the written permission of the authors.
Published by Notorious USA

Introduction

Welcome to another in our series of books about the country's most infamous crimes. Some Notorious U.S.A. crimes you have followed over the years, and some may be new to you.

If you're reading this, you probably have an uneasy fascination with murder, as we do. It attracts and repels us. We recoil with shock and horror from some murders. Some—admit it—we are entertained by. Others we struggle to understand. Who were these people? What motivated them to commit murder? Did they 'snap'? Could they be innocent? And what do we know *now* about a crime that occurred years ago?

When we take another look at crimes and notorious criminals—living or deceased—we learn more about what made them tick, about their crimes, and about their victims.

There's no expiration date on our fascination with twisted people who commit twisted crimes.

In Notorious Mississippi we learn about a love triangle gone bad; how greed can lead all too easily to murder; the lengths one woman went to in order to get rid of her mother; and the latest on an especially heinous crime, Shaken Baby Syndrome.

Let us know if there is a case you would like to read more about.

—Gregg Olsen, Olalla, Washington
—Rebecca Morris, Seattle, Washington

Black Widow in a Pure White Dress

Stephanie Stevens

WHEN KAREN STEPHENS ANSWERED HER TELEPHONE one February day in 1995, she heard what no wife wants to hear—the voice of her husband's much younger mistress. Stephanie Tate-Kennedy was a nurse at the hospital where Karen's husband, Dr. David Stephens, worked as a surgeon, and they'd been carrying on a relationship for months. According to accounts from David and Karen's daughter, Kristen Stephens, her mother had been suspicious of David for a few months, but she wasn't sure who he might be seeing. Thanks to the phone call, Karen's fears were confirmed. After more than 30 years of marriage, David had found someone else.

For Karen, the affair was a devastating blow. The Stephens' were high school sweethearts who married young in 1960 (seven years before David's new lover was even born) and raised two children together. They were two of the most well-known and respected members of their Hattiesburg, Mississippi community. They'd moved there from Georgia in the mid 1980's so that David could help establish a heart clinic at Forrest General Hospital, and over the past decade he'd become Chief of Surgery and sat as a board member at the hospital and at the local university. If David left Karen for this other woman, everything they'd built together would crumble.

Karen hung up the phone and confronted her husband. An argument ensued, and as it began to unravel, David headed outside. Desperate to capture her husband's attention—perhaps afraid he might drive off for good—Karen grabbed a gun from inside the house and ran to the driveway holding it to her mouth. Then, in a cruel twist of fate, Karen tripped, accidentally firing the weapon and shooting herself in the mouth. The gunshot left her paralyzed from the neck down, and after two months in the hospital, Karen's ventilator failed, leaving her dead at the age of 50. Karen's death was ruled a suicide, despite David's argument that the gun firing was an accident.

David made his career and his millions as a successful heart surgeon, but he'd lost his own wife to a broken heart. Hers.

It's tempting to speculate about what was said over the phone the day Karen died. If the mistress' call was simply a case of bad timing, then why didn't Stephanie just hang up when David didn't answer? Did the caller confront Karen intentionally or say something to put her over the edge? The only two women who could have answered that question were Karen Stephens and her husband's lover, Stephanie Tate-Kennedy.

Stephanie was a wife and mother of two in her early 20's when she began working as an operating room nurse at Forrest General Hospital. She'd spent her teens as a pageant queen in Louisiana, married before the age of 18, and moved to Mississippi for nursing school. In an episode of the television series *American Justice*, a former co-worker of Stephanie's recalls her saying, "I'm going to catch me a doctor." The woman knew Stephanie was already married and had children, but Stephanie didn't seem to think that was much of a complication.

Not long after she'd arrived at Forrest General, Stephanie zeroed in on David Stephens. He was successful, wealthy, and still good-looking despite being 25 years her senior. David didn't seem to mind gaining the attention of an attractive, young nurse, and before long the couple's not-so-secret flirtation at work evolved into a full-blown affair. Even after Karen's accident, Stephanie stood by to comfort David while Karen lay paralyzed in the hospital. After Karen died, David and Stephanie began dating publicly. They wasted little time, and in May 1996, the couple exchanged vows in a ceremony at the Stephens' home, *Stephanie's* home now.

AT FIRST, LIFE AS A SURGEON'S WIFE WAS A DREAM FOR STEPHANIE STEPHENS. She quickly settled into her new charmed life, buying a new car, fine jewelry, and anything else her heart desired. Stephanie's reputation in town was badly tarnished, as many knew of the affair and the death of David's first wife, but that didn't seem to bother her. In fact, Stephanie devoted her energy to designing a brand new home for her and David: a custom Mississippi mansion conveniently located right next to the Hattiesburg Country Club. Some of Stephanie's biggest critics were now her closest neighbors. For now, Stephanie had a doctor's ring on her finger and a surgeon's salary at her disposal. It wouldn't last long.

David and Stephanie were just settling into life as a married couple when their luck took a steep downward spiral. By the late 1990's, David began experiencing major health issues. Years earlier he'd been diagnosed with Hepatitis C, but hadn't experienced any serious symptoms. Suddenly, he was very ill and the treatment he underwent left him with a badly damaged liver. In addition, David was diagnosed with diabetes. He was required to wear an insulin pump at all times, and the combined effects of diabetes and Hepatitis C left him unable to perform as a surgeon. David's illness was enough to effectively end his medical career. He was left with only part-time work assessing medical records; it was a far cry from the life and salary he'd grown accustomed to. Meanwhile, Stephanie had health problems of her own. A car accident left her crippled with a broken hip, and Crohn's disease affected her digestive tract. While Stephanie helped care for David, the couple also hired a nanny for Stephanie's two daughters and an in-home nurse.

Some might call it karma. Only a few years into their marriage, Stephanie and David found themselves both unable to work and increasingly unable to enjoy the luxuries that go along with making millions.

IN THE MEDICAL PROFESSION, A GUIDING PRINCIPAL IS TO FIRST, DO NO HARM. Unfortunately for Dr. David Stephens, the nurse he fell in love with had her own set of principles.

On May 1, 2001, almost exactly six years after the death of his first wife Karen, David died in bed at his Hattiesburg mansion. Stephanie reported the death, telling authorities that she'd woken up late that morning and realized that David, who was lying beside her, was dead. She took his pulse to be sure, and then called the town coroner, Butch Benedict. He arrived to find Stephanie distraught and still in bed next to David. As he helped Stephanie remove David's insulin pump, Butch watched her place two vials in her pocket. If Stephanie's behavior seemed a bit strange at the time, it still didn't raise any major red flags. While tragic for his family, David's death wasn't entirely surprising. After all, he'd been ill for some time and his liver was getting worse by the day. It appeared that at the age of 59, David's illness had finally gotten the best of him. Still, as a precaution, the coroner wanted to check for a possible insulin overdose. He asked his deputy to collect a blood sample from David's body before the burial. It was a fairly standard procedure that would yield unlikely results.

Stephanie, now a widow, was left to grieve the loss of her second husband and the life she'd hoped they might share together. Almost immediately, Stephanie's actions left friends and family wondering if there was more to the story. David's daughter Kristen, who already disliked Stephanie, became certain after her father died that Stephanie was up to something. After arriving in Hattiesburg for David's funeral, Kristen entered David and Stephanie's bedroom and discovered a pile of financial documents spread around the bed.

"Who would be reading that sort of stuff, not even 24 hours after their husband died?" Kristen said in an interview with the television series *48 Hours*.

A few weeks later, lab results from David's blood test came back. The toxicology report showed traces of Etomidate, an anesthetic typically used during short surgeries. There was no reason for such a drug to be in David's bloodstream, and the finding persuaded a judge to have David's body exhumed for further testing. Meanwhile, the Hattiesburg Police Department decided to ask Stephanie if she knew anything about Etomidate or how it wound up in David's body. Stephanie told authorities she know nothing about the emergency room anesthetic. Coming from a registered nurse like Stephanie, this didn't make any sense. She was either poorly trained or not telling the truth.

Further tests on David's body screened positive for

another hospital-grade drug known as Atracurium. A muscle relaxant, Atracurium is typically used to stop a patients' breathing during surgery. Without life support, the drug will quickly cause a patient to suffocate.

Investigators concluded that the Atracurium and Etomidate must have been administered via David's insulin pump. As she faced more and more questions, Stephanie told authorities that David became deeply depressed over his illness and the loss of his career. She insinuated that her husband might have even been suicidal. Still, police and David's family dismissed Stephanie's claims. For Kristen, it was simply not fathomable that her father would kill himself.

"It wasn't possible, having known my father, for that ever to be an option," Kristen later testified. "I don't care what kind of evidence you have."

Investigators had their own reasons to doubt the suicide theory. The drugs that killed David are typically so fast-acting that it would have been almost impossible for him to have administered them and cleaned up before their effects set in. Still, it was possible that outside of an emergency room, the drugs may have acted more slowly, giving David more time if, in fact, he was committing suicide.

The drugs left some room for debate as to whether David died at his own hand or someone else's, but a piece of paper found in Stephanie and David's home screamed foul play. While searching the house, a lead detective on the case discovered a form from David's pension fund. Apparently MetLife received a request for the document, which allowed David to cash out his $732,000 savings fund. David signed off on the payout on April 30, one day before he died. This was out of the ordinary, as David had received the form and declined to collect the payout several times in the past.

Further investigation revealed that, according to MetLife, the form wasn't sent until May 1, and by then of course, David was already dead. Someone must have forged David's signature.

Meanwhile, as Hattiesburg authorities worked David's case, Stephanie was busy enjoying whirlwind shopping sprees and falling in love—again. David had been dead for barely a year when Stephanie flew off to Vegas in June 2002 for her third walk down the aisle, this time with a 29-year-old handyman named Chris Watts. Ever the generous bride, Stephanie footed the bill for the couple and two close friends to fly round-trip to Las Vegas and spend four weeks at the luxurious Venetian Hotel. During the vacation the couple burned through the entire $80,000 annuity Stephanie received from her late husband's estate. It was a final big blowout for a couple that would soon be lucky if they ever got a conjugal visit.

NOTHING PLEASES A COURTROOM LIKE A BLACK WIDOW IN A PURE WHITE DRESS.

Pearls draped her neck and studded her ears, offsetting her dark eyes and raven hair. The look was appropriate for a woman who always did love playing the part of a new bride. She'd been arrested a year earlier, only two months after her marriage to Chris. As luck would have it, Stephanie's new husband couldn't attend her trial because he was already behind bars. Chris was serving time for attempting to have one of his ex-girlfriends murdered. He was doomed to spend the first years of his marriage in a cell, and now Stephanie—only a few days from her 36th birthday—was looking at a similar fate.

The Stephanie Stephens trial was the first case in Mississippi to allow cameras in the courtroom. Stephanie was already one of the most controversial women in Hattiesburg, but now she would stand judgment before the entire country. Stephanie's defense team argued that David Stephens—severely depressed by his terminal illness—was suicidal. The prosecution maintained that Stephanie was not only a home wrecker, but also a calculated and manipulative seductress who poisoned her own husband to get his money.

As luck would have it, one of the state's key witnesses was Stephanie's former friend, Karen Burnett. Karen—one of the two friends Stephanie took on her Las Vegas wedding trip—testified that on the day of the wedding, the bride confessed that she'd given David two sedatives to help him end his life. While her testimony played a major role in the state's case, Karen's story was weakened by yet another strange turn of events in Stephanie's unlucky life. Shortly after David's death, Stephanie's home was burglarized. Some of the missing items were later found in a storage locker registered to Karen, and while Karen denied any involvement in the burglary, Stephanie's defense team claimed that Karen may have avoided charges related to the theft by agreeing to testify at Stephanie's trial.

In the end, the state's case had the upper hand. Between her access to the emergency room drugs found in David's body, the forged MetLife form, and her serious spending habit, Stephanie had too many factors stacked against her to give jurors any reasonable doubt that she killed her husband. She was convicted of first-degree murder and sentenced to life in prison, effectively ending her days as a wealthy widow for good. Once the verdict was announced, David's daughter Kristen Stephens exchanged emotional hugs with loved ones, thanking them for their support. She turned to the cameras, triumphantly proclaiming, "Justice has been served."

Stephanie would have been 65 years old by the time she became eligible for parole, but that day never came. After serving only three years of her sentence, she died on October 14, 2006 of double pneumonia in a hospital near Jackson, Miss. She was 39 years old. Meanwhile, Kristen went home to raise her own two children, a girl and a boy named Karen and David after her parents.

The Good Daughter

The Story of Ouida Keeton

TINY BRANCHES CLAWED AT OUIDA KEETON'S COLD, PALE LEGS as she lugged two heavy bundles through the woods.

Searching for a place to hide the stark white packages amongst the forest's earthy browns and greens, Ouida realized she should have tossed the packages into the water and let them wash out to sea. Searing pains shot up and down her back as she wavered under the 70-pound load. Her feet heavy with mud and weeds clumped to the sides of her dainty shoes, she finally dropped the bundles to the ground with an unceremonious thud. Inside, swaddled like a pair of newborns in cloths and old sugar sacks, was a pair of butchered human legs, chopped at the hips and again below the knees. They were all that remained of Ouida's mother.

It was Monday, January 21st, 1935, in the dead of Mississippi's short but temperamental winter. Icy raindrops burst from the sky, making long trails down Ouida's forehead and cheeks as she scurried back toward her car. She stepped in, sitting on copies of the *New York Times* she'd used to line the seats and floorboards, and stepped hard on the gas. With an ominous grinding noise, the vehicle jolted in place, flinging mud against the sides of the doors and tires. Of all the goddamn days to get her car stuck, she thought, this was not the one.

Ouida made it six miles by foot through sleet and rain down Highway 11 before a kind stranger named W.E. Kennedy stopped to pick her up, agreeing to drop her off in the nearby town of Laurel. Figuring she owed him some explanation for her being barelegged in the middle of nowhere on a stormy morning, Ouida murmured something about visiting an old woman while her mother was in New Orleans. Then, turning her head so Kennedy wouldn't see her face, she confessed, "I'm just completely given out, just a nervous wreck." It was one of the last honest things she'd say for a long time to come.

DURING THE EARLY 1900'S, THE DELTA TOWN OF LAUREL, Mississippi was best known for its booming lumber industry. Located in a region known as the Pine Belt, the town used its dual train tracks to ship and mill more yellow pine than any other area in the world. As the industry grew, local farmers and blue-collar workers found themselves rubbing elbows with an increasingly wealthy business class.

Even among the upper crust of new money moguls, the Keeton family stood apart, both for their wealth and their terminal dysfunction. Despite her short stature, Daisy McKinsey Keeton, the family matriarch, was a force to be reckoned with. In matters of finance and family, she was uncompromising and occasionally domineering. Her four children, Maude, Ouida, Earl, and Eloise, fed the town gossip mills for years with one scandalous outburst after another.

They arrived in Laurel in 1913, on the heels of a birth, a death and a windfall. The birth was to Daisy's youngest child, Eloise, and the death and the windfall that followed came when Ouida's father, John Monroe Keeton, died in a mysterious railroad accident. Having several life insurance policies and a double indemnity clause conveniently in place, John Keeton left behind a sizable fortune for his wife and children. Daisy, newly widowed, moved the family 100 miles from the tiny town of McNeil, Miss. to a an affluent neighborhood in Laurel.

Despite the charmed life the insurance money lent them—possibly because of it—the wayward Keeton children and their controlling mother couldn't seem to stay out of trouble in their new town.

Earl, Daisy's only son, had several run-ins with the law as a young man. In addition to being accused of gang rape, he stood by as his close friend shot and killed a well-known attorney named Burns Deavours during a petty scuffle outside a local bar.

Eloise, bold and independent from an early age, pulled the entire family into a highly publicized lawsuit by age 18. Without her mother's blessing, she and a young man named Rayburn Robinson eloped and fled town. Predictably, Daisy reeled against her daughter's disobedient behavior, convincing local authorities to track the young newlyweds down. Claiming Eloise was not yet of marrying age (though she had to be at least 18 as she was born before her father's death in 1907) Daisy saw to it that her daughter returned to Laurel. When Eloise's groom came after his pretty bride only to be turned away, he fired back with a lawsuit naming Daisy, the Keeton children, Maude's husband David McRae, and family friend W. M. Carter, in a lawsuit for alienation of affection. While charges against the rest of the family were quickly dropped, Daisy and Robinson remained in a nasty legal battle for several years.

While Earl and Eloise were both handfuls, the older siblings, Maude and Ouida, were generally well-behaved.

Though Maude and her mother butted heads often, she and her husband stayed close to home and helped Ouida by allowing her to work at McRae's filling station (which they owned and operated) after she stopped working for Carter. Ouida, quiet and aloof but also witty and attractive, maintained a positive public persona by keeping her many quirks deep under wraps. While outsiders admired Ouida's lavish wardrobe and thick, raven curls, those close to her knew she was slightly obsessed with her image. At times, she spent hours gazing before her mirror, primping and painting her angular face to perfection. In her thirties, after gaining a bit of weight, she became obsessed with thinning down, using a "reducing machine" and taking frequent trips to the hot springs for spa treatments. Neighbors noticed her rapidly diminishing weight during the two years prior to Daisy's murder and wondered if her health was in peril.

Ouida's other secret was far more explosive and heavily guarded. She and William Madison Carter, the much older married man (at least three decades Ouida's senior) who became a close Keeton family friend, quietly carried on a love affair for years under Daisy's nose. Carter, who employed Ouida when she was 17 (and he was in his fifties), was a prominent and well-respected lumber mogul. His affections for his secretary began not long after he hired her and spanned years, even as Ouida left her position with him, traveled to Washington D.C. for schooling, and returned home with news of her engagement. He made frequent nightly visits to Daisy and Ouida, chatting before Daisy's fireplace for hours and tucking love notes in the sofa cushions for her daughter to find.

While most of the relationship took place while Carter was married, he became free to take up with a new woman after his wife, Nettie, died in 1933. Rather than seizing the opportunity to legitimize his relationship with Ouida, Carter continued to veil his affections, as if he were ashamed of the romance. Going a step further, he introduced Ouida to a nurse from Mobile named Harriet Adams, the other woman he'd secretly taken up with. Only Ouida knew of the secret mailbox he kept, sending Harriet letters disguised with a fake name.

At one point, Carter and Harriet were involved in an auto accident while in Laurel. Carter asked Ouida to claim Harriet as a houseguest to avoid suspicion as she recovered. For years Ouida went along, keeping Carter's secrets and agreeing to remain his woman on the side. Deep down she must have wanted more, and unbeknownst to Carter she had her own secret. Stored away in her dresser drawers, out of sight but never out of mind, were tiny clothes made to fit a newborn. How many times had she peeked at them, longingly knowing that for all his poems and gifts, Carter would never give her a family?

Until the end of her life, Daisy remained unaware of Ouida and Carter's relationship. As far as Daisy was concerned, she alone held Ouida's unwavering loyalty and devotion. Outsiders marveled at the mother-daughter duo as they passed hours chatting and laughing on the porch swing beneath the starry southern sky. Even in her most guarded matters—those of her finances—Daisy's trust in her middle daughter was unshakable. As Robinson's lawsuit loomed, Daisy looked to Carter for advice and wisdom in protecting her fortune. Her solution, perhaps at Carter's suggestion, was to transfer the entire estate—including her house, money, and assets—into Ouida's name for safekeeping. It was an ill-fated decision to say the least.

DAN EVANS JR. NOTICED SOMETHING ON THE GROUND

while walking through the woods one rainy Monday. A local farmer who'd lived near Sandersville all his life, Evans was out rabbit hunting around noon with his dogs. A few yards off of the highway they became distracted, sniffing and growling at something lying in the middle of the ground. Evans ventured closer to inspect and had the shock of his life. "I walked on up there and saw there was some flesh in them," Evans later testified. "I got a stick and rolled one of them over and discovered it wasn't hog or beef flesh, but human flesh."

Mortified, the black farmer hurried home to tell his wife and others about the macabre discovery. Eventually, word made its way to Griffin Cook, a constable for Jasper County. By mid-afternoon, he and several other officials stood flabbergasted, ignorant of the cold and snow. What in the world to make of some poor woman's butchered and abandoned body parts?

Within a matter of hours the story was circulating through town. Curious locals and reporters swarmed the secluded crime-scene even as an evening snowstorm blew in. Cook earned the abhorrent task of driving the thighs to the Sumrall Funeral Home, gagging over the wretched smell of rotting human flesh. At the funeral home, the legs were preserved, weighed, and photographed. The hunt was on to find the rest of the mysterious slain woman and her madman butcher-assailant.

By Tuesday morning the "legs" story made its print debut. The local paper, the *Laurel Leader-Call*, included a photo with Evans—referred to as a "negro rabbit hunter"—and his dogs posing in front of the dumping site. The following day, Wednesday, Jan. 23rd. Carter made his first visit to the Keeton home since Daisy's murder. He'd been out of town since early Sunday morning visiting Harriet

Adams in Mobile, but couldn't help stopping by to see his other favorite girl. As Ouida walked up her driveway, carrying a jar of milk, Carter hopped out of his car and tossed a snowball gently toward her face. Perhaps he hoped to break the tension that jumping between lovers can cause. The Keeton's neighbor, Cammie Cook, looked on from her porch as the two peculiarly avoided the house, instead chatting for about an hour in the front of Carter's parked Pontiac. It was the last conversation they'd have before both fought for their lives and reputations. Tellingly, Ouida was sitting in the driver's seat.

As papers churned out details of the discovery, two men found themselves recalling their encounters with a nervous, beautiful girl the previous Monday morning. Kennedy, the city worker who gave Ouida a ride from Sandersville, and W.P. Duckworth, a garage man who helped her go back to retrieve her car, both contacted authorities when they realized they'd probably aided a criminal. By Friday morning, three officials paid a visit to the Keeton home. Laurel Police Chief Jim Brown knocked at Daisy's door as Jones County Chief Deputy Sherriff, J.C. Hamilton, and Jones County Attorney, Jack Deavours (younger brother of the attorney Earl's friend killed years earlier), waited patiently outside.

Brown, who'd known the Keeton family from Eloise's lawsuit years earlier, entered the home cordially and asked Ouida if he might speak with her mother. She explained that Daisy was in New Orleans visiting Eloise, and perhaps sensing that her word might be in question, offered to produce a letter Daisy sent her while on the trip. Not surprisingly, after a moment of looking around she apologized to Brown that she must have simply misplaced it. Scanning the room, Brown noticed three carving knives left dirty on the counter. On a shelf he also spied a stack of folded cloths, not unlike the ones used to wrap the abandoned legs. In the bathroom, Brown thought he heard some water running. He walked in and realized the tub was turned up full blast with the drain removed, as if to flush something away.

With a bit more gentle prodding, Brown asked finally Ouida if she'd ride with him downtown. She agreed, and soon found herself sitting in Deavours' office for a slightly less friendly interrogation. Brown would find far more troubling evidence when he returned to the house later that afternoon, searching the premises under Earl's supervision. Daisy's only son hadn't heard from his mother in several days. He was as eager as anyone to find out if Daisy was living or dead.

During her multiple interviews with Deavours, Ouida offered many attempts at explaining her mother's disappearance and the witnesses who claimed they saw her the morning the legs were found. One of her most colorful tales involved an elderly woman in a bonnet and several men with guns blindfolding Ouida and kidnapping her mother for $10,000 ransom. For hours she sat in Deavours' office, her siblings at her side, as she offered other unlikely iterations of her mother's supposed kidnapping. Finally, exhausted and perhaps thinking of Carter's words as they sat in his car, *Harriet sends her regards,* Ouida cracked, telling Deavours, "Mother was standing by the fireplace and he struck her down with the iron poker."

He, Ouida claimed, was the well-known businessman W.M. Carter.

Ouida and Deavours went back and forth, going over and over the facts. The confession Ouida finally signed was mostly fabricated, with a few honest details sprinkled in for good measure. There was a brief argument between Daisy and Carter, she said, that took place early Saturday night, January 21st in Daisy's bedroom. Suddenly, as her mother stood to pour brandy in a glass on the mantle, Carter struck Daisy over the head with the fire poker. He hit her several more times on the floor before forcing Ouida, under threat of violence, to help carry Daisy's body out to his Pontiac.

Daisy said that Carter returned later saying something about putting the body in a box—except there hadn't been room for her mother's legs. He suggested she dump them over a bridge into the river.

But Carter testified he was out of town when all that happened. Public opinion was that Ouida had cut up her mother in the bathtub. Regardless of who did what—there were legs to be disposed of.

After a short trip, Ouida claimed, Carter returned and mentioned something about putting the body in a box. He instructed Ouida to help him carry the legs back into the house, then suggested she should dump them over a bridge into the river. By dawn, Carter left for Mobile, and when he arrived back in town Wednesday, he was angered by the papers' news of legs being discovered in the woods.

After reprimanding her for her carelessness, it was he, Ouida said, who dreamed up the wacky kidnapping story about the old woman in the bonnet. In this nuanced rendition of the story, Ouida offered up plenty of dirt on Carter for Deavours to uncover during a trial. She volunteered Carter's secret affair with Harriet, even disclosing the location of the confidential mailbox he'd kept for years. She explained away Carter's lack of motive saying simply, "He wanted me to have more privileges."

Carter, in turn, was arrested two days after Ouida. Hoping to avoid any disclosure of his love affairs, he claimed he'd been in Mobile for business and knew nothing of the wretched murder. He also, initially, skipped over his meeting with Ouida, a portion of her story that witnesses had already backed up. While Carter's motive in changing his story was likely to avoid rumors of philandering, the omissions made Ouida's accusations seem possible. She had him trapped; he was forced to either appear guilty of a hideous crime or obliterate his public persona by using his mistress as an alibi.

It's hard to think this wasn't a brilliantly calculated choice on Ouida's part. She knew the lengths he'd gone to keep his relationship with Harriet private for so long, and that without disclosing the trip it'd be hard to get through Deavours' merciless probing. Scorned for her rival, could Ouida have used her predicament to give Carter a taste of poetic justice?

Investigators sensed that something was missing from both stories. Hoping to illicit some outburst of truth, they arranged for Ouida to visit Carter at the Hinds County jail in Jackson. Sitting face to face with Carter, Ouida made no effort to recant. She literally pointed a shaky finger at the man she claimed was responsible for taking her beloved mother's life. The following day she collapsed with a nervous breakdown, embarking on an ongoing limbo between hospital rooms and jail cells.

BALIFFS RUSHED TO CLEAR THE OVERCROWDED JONES COUNTY courtroom in fear that the balcony might come crashing to the ground any minute.

Covering the first day of testimony of the highly anticipated "Legs" trial, the *Leader-Call* reported, "Several hundred lives were endangered including between two and three hundred seated upstairs and as many more under the balcony." The article later noted that in one area, the balcony had already sunk nearly 12 inches before it was vacated. Had Judge W. Joe Pack not insisted on delaying the proceedings that morning, it's possible one of the most infamous murder trials in the South's history would have turned into a tragedy of much greater proportion.

Onlookers pushing their way into the courtroom were already up to date on nearly every development in the state's case against the now infamous Ouida Keeton. Papers printed multiple stories every day on the beauty accused of helping slaughter her own kin. The stories outlined Ouida's eventful Monday morning off the highway, her accusations against Carter, her involvement in Eloise's lawsuit, and even the fact that she'd taken butchery lessons (she earned all A's) while enrolled in hotel management courses in Washington D.C. Attending Ouida's trial offered spectators a real-life window into their favorite new murder mystery.

Providing all the drama anyone could have hoped for, a nurse wheeled Ouida's withering body into the courthouse. Frail, thin, and slightly aged looking, but comely nonetheless, she was a caricature of a tragic, forlorn, damsel. While bouncing in and out of the hospital over the previous weeks, she'd eventually gone completely mute. Now, resting in her wheelchair, she appeared nearly catatonic.

The first five witnesses—including Kennedy, Duckworth, Evans, Cook, and a farmer named Will Saul who saw Ouida's car Monday morning—served to place Ouida and the legs in the woods the morning of January 21st. Canny reporters noticed the single tear rolling down Ouida's cheek during Kennedy's testimony. It was one of the only emotional clues she'd offer through the entirety of her trial.

Attendees continued to swarm the courtroom each day for new tales of love and murder at the house on the corner of Cross Street. Packing lunches and cross-stitching projects so they could settle in for hours of testimony at a time, townspeople sat wide eyed as testimony grew more and more eerie.

During one session, several of the Keeton's neighbors recalled a smell similar to burning hair or rubber blowing from the corner of Cross Street the Sunday and Monday after Daisy's murder. While most of them couldn't quite pinpoint the awful smell, a key witness named Virgil Sumrall said he'd recognized the odor from past experience. "It was in the Canal Zone, at the crematory, where they burn bodies," Sumrall recalled while questioned by District Attorney Alexander Currie. At another point, Ouida casually dozed off leaning back in her wheelchair as jurors cringed, passing around photos of Daisy's severed thighs. The most striking piece of evidence, by far, were the legs themselves, brought in by the local undertaker in a small case for the jury and a few officials in the front of the courtroom to queasily view. Attendees in the balcony squirmed forward, hoping they might get a look.

Chief Brown, who'd uncovered most of the evidence, offered the jury a laundry list of the grim artifacts he found while searching the Keeton home. There was a pair of gray stockings that he pulled from Ouida's fireplace, as well as her dainty suede shoes (not in the fireplace), which both gave off a particularly vile odor. He'd found blood on the right side of Daisy's bed and splattered near the mantle, which Ouida confessed to painting to cover the stains. He recalled the bathwater, explaining, "The water was running out of the faucet and going out as fast as it come in." The jury knew there'd also been blood smeared and speckled in the bathroom, and, while nothing was said outright, the underlying idea was that parts of the body were butchered, discarded, or both, in the tub.

As the second portion of the trial began, Ouida's defense team, faced with too much evidence to rebut, worked to convince the jury their client was insane. The "evidence" they provided, while compelling, wouldn't live up to today's scientific standards. Acquaintances and some family members commented that there was just something in her eyes, or she recently seemed a bit "off". She had grown thin and was known to occasionally sit gazing into her mirror for hours at a time. Specialists, in turn, said Ouida lacked reflexes. Referencing tests involving needles and feathers, they explained that Ouida no longer reacted to anything. While her behavior in the courtroom seemed to demonstrate that she was, in fact, "off", an unplanned moment outside the courthouse cast doubt (and a healthy dose of comic relief) on the defense's case. *The Miami News* published an amusing account of the incident headlined, "The Pretty Murderess Who Was Too Modest."

Woman's oldest virtue—modesty—consists of a set of reflexes to which many young women relate automatically, even in the ultra-sophisticated era of abbreviated bathing suits, daring evening gowns, and nudism. One day, as a deputy wheeled Ouida across the courthouse lawn to a waiting car, there came a fickle breeze rippling through the elms and live oaks. It bellowed back the skirts of the woman reclining in the wheel chair, revealing an immodest display of shapely, silk shod limbs. As if by magic Ouida snapped out of her coma, sat up straight to yank down those unruly skirts, and then sank back quickly on her blankets.

Aside from the question of Ouida's sanity, three mysteries threaded their way through the trial, complicating the jury's already difficult decision. First, there was the murder itself. While some facts were apparent—the crime took place in the Keeton home between Saturday night and Sunday morning, the body was butchered and portions were burned, and Ouida took part in the disposal—conflicting evidence left the exact nature of Daisy's death unknown.

Blood on the mantle and poker backed up Ouida's story that her mother took a deadly blow while standing over the fireplace. But Brown also found a gun in Ouida's drawers (stolen from McRae's filling station where Ouida worked for her brother-in-law) with three of its six chambers spent. Neighbors testified to hearing gunshots sometime after midnight, casting doubt on Ouida's claim that only the poker was used and the crime took place around 8 p.m.

There were also large blood stains on Daisy's bed and pillow that hinted at the possibility she was shot in her sleep. Was she killed with the poker or was she shot? Was it Carter, Ouida, or both? What happened to the rest of the body? These questions hung like a thick humid haze over the proceedings.

Even more fascinating was the problem of corpus delicti. Latin for "body of crime," corpus delicti is the principal that in order to be convicted of a crime (murder), there must be evidence that the crime actually took place (a body). While today's sophisticated crime labs could easily test whether the blood and body parts found by authorities actually belonged to Daisy Keeton, the best investigators could do in the 1930's was to have chemists testify that the red stains and oily splotches they found were, in fact, from a human body. (The oil, it was said, was a fatty substance that resulted from burning human flesh.) While there was strong probable evidence that the legs did belong to Daisy

Keeton, there was no way to definitively prove anything.

In the end, the jury found Ouida guilty of slaughtering her mother, but didn't have the heart to see her hang. On March 12, 1925, they compromised with a life sentence.

The verdict appeared in papers around the country, immortalizing Ouida as a strange and monstrous murderer. *The Spartanburg Herald* in South Carolina described Ouida's reaction, writing, "The slender, pallid defendant heard the verdict from her wheelchair without any visible reaction, nor did she display any emotion when Judge W. Joe Pack pronounced the sentence."

Judge Pack took mercy on Ouida's pitiful state and granted her bail at $15,000. She sought shelter with her sister, Maude, and her family as she awaited her appeal and prepared to testify at Carter's trial.

A little more than two months after she'd sat indifferently while a jury sentenced her to life, Ouida was suddenly almost as good as her old self. She was still thin and had aged considerably, but in her chic silk dress and matching hat she was once more a woman to envy.

The courtroom and the country held their breath while she sauntered toward the witness stand. While she'd never spoken a word at her own trial, her strength retuned just in time to testify against Carter. Sitting only a few feet away, Carter stared into the eyes of a woman he'd been close to for more than a decade. Outwardly she remained lovely, but Carter knew by now that she was a predator who'd chosen him for prey. After having her fragile heart toyed with until there was practically none of it left, Ouida returned from the dead as Carter's own personal poltergeist. She testified:

The 1 o'clock train going north had gone up   I let him in the side window   He had only been in my room a very short time when he heard a slight noise in Mother's room and he ran in there and I heard shots fired and I went into the room and Mother—I sat down on the side of Mother's bed and tried to get her to speak to me and she wouldn't. While I was sitting there holding her—the man I thought was always my friend started abusing me and said 'Get up or I will do to you just what I did to your mother.' I went all to pieces and I don't remember anything else.

Listening intently, those who'd been following the story since the beginning realized this was not the same story they'd heard before. In this version, Carter shot Daisy in her bed. The fact that Ouida remained an innocent victim, however, was still part of the story. During his questioning, Currie covered a spectrum of events including Ouida's employment and resulting relationship with Carter, the day and night of Daisy's murder, and Ouida and Carter's meeting the Wednesday after.

Then, introducing Rayburn Robinson's lawsuit, Currie touched on something that didn't get much attention at Ouida's own trial: motive.

Currie: Is the defendant, W.M. Carter, the man named as a co-defendant in this lawsuit the same W.M. Carter who was jointly indicted for the murder of Mrs. Daisy Keeton?

Ouida: Yes.

Currie: I will ask you to state if in the progress of that lawsuit whether money belonging to Mrs. Daisy Keeton was turned over to you and deposited by you to your credit in the banks.

Ouida: It was.

Currie: State whether or not, if you know, the defendant W.M. Carter was personally familiar with every item and detail of the personal affairs of Mrs. Daisy Keeton.

The defense objected but Currie eventually followed through with his line of questioning.

Currie: Then describe just what his relationship has been toward the family in a business way, how you have looked upon him?

Ouida: We have gone to him for everything, looked upon his advice as being absolutely perfect.

Currie: At the time of this litigation suit I mentioned were you in his employ?

Ouida: I was.

Currie: Miss Ouida, is your mother now living or dead?

Ouida: She is dead.

In essence, Ouida had control of her mother's fortune, and based on her statements, Carter had knowledge of the situation as well as influence over Daisy. Working together, there may have been an opportunity for the seasoned businessman and his young lover, who after years of obedience was eager to break free of her mother's chains. Perhaps because Ouida herself was no longer on trial, Currie failed to neatly connect his points by adding that Daisy had recently talked with her daughter about reclaiming her funds. She no longer wished to need her daughter's permission to sign all her own checks. If Ouida wanted to keep a grip on Daisy's money, she knew the window was closing.

The trial continued, with Carter continually exposed to an array of public humiliations. He'd secretly run around with Harriet even as his sick wife was dying; had at least a flirtation and at most a long term sexual affair with his secretary; and might have committed a ghastly murder. Rather than using her energy to save herself, Ouida employed all her will and wit in service of Carter's demise. On June 6, 1935, thanks in great part to Ouida's testimony; Carter received his own lifetime sentence behind bars.

WHILE OUIDA NEVER OUTLIVED HER SENTENCE AS A MURDERESS, the Supreme Court overturned Carter's sentence, and he had a second trial.

Preparing for round two, Deavours asked Ouida if she'd retell her story. After marinating on the matter, Ouida reversed her position. She didn't claim Carter was innocent, but she told Deavours she could no longer be sure she remembered anything she'd said. Without her testimony, the case against Carter was paper-thin.

Carter, after a rough tumble through the justice system, eventually was a free man. Even a reversed sentence, however, couldn't repair his sullied reputation. Never again would his business boom like it once had, and while his family stood by his side, they must not have been able to look at him quite the same. To this day, it is unclear if Carter committed a villainous deed against his close friend, or if he was entrapped by his young, scorned lover. In his book, *The Legs Murder Scandal*, which offers an incredibly in depth exploration of the case, author Hunter Cole reveals that based on the evidence, Carter was likely not around the evening of Daisy's murder.

As for Ouida, the courts maintained that she was certainly guilty of *something*. Her stay in the penitentiary was awful but brief. On April 17th an examining physician at Parchman Detention Farm, where Ouida experienced regular vomiting and listlessness, concluded that the frail felon was unfit for life behind bars. To her family's delight, and probably her own relief, she was eventually transferred to Whitfield State Hospital.

On Tuesday, March 26, the infamous legs of the "legs murder" were buried in the family Keeton plot. In a perfect cosmic twist, the burial—attended by none of the Keeton children—coincided with Ouida's birthday. Many years later, on November 11, 1973, Ouida died at the age of 74. After such a gruesome and fascinating life something as matter-of-fact as pneumonia ended her life.

No obituary made the *Laurel Leader-Call*, or any newspaper in the area, and no extravagant tomb announced her grave. Anyone curious enough, however, can find a pair of unfussy slabs side by side in McNeil Cemetery where, just as Daisy would want, she and Ouida remain forever inseparable.

The Murderous Middle School Teacher

Carla Ann Hughes

HER EARS STILL BUZZING FROM HOURS OF TODDLER CHITTER-CHATTER, Avis Banks wearily climbed into her car and pulled the seatbelt over her growing belly.

It was November 29, 2006, and the holiday season was in full swing. After a nice, long Thanksgiving weekend it was hard to get back into the grind of the workweek, and being five months pregnant didn't make things any easier. Worn out as she was, Avis loved her job as a daycare worker, loved getting to see her family for the holidays, and loved that growing belly and all the promise of a loving family it held. With one aching foot she pushed on the gas pedal, beginning the route toward her Ridgeland, Miss. home, a town of about 24,000 people just a few miles north of the capital, Jackson.

At 5:36 p.m., Avis, 25 years old, dialed her husband-to-be, letting him know she was on her way home. Thirty-one year old Keyon Pittman was in the middle of coaching basketball practice and wouldn't be home for a while, but Avis liked to check in now and then just the same. When she pulled into her subdivision around 5:50 p.m., strings of white Christmas lights twinkled against her red brick house, illuminating a small wreath hung on the door. Soon, Avis and Keyon would celebrate their first Christmas in the new house, and by the next year, they'd celebrate as a family:

husband, wife, and their tiny baby.

Before going into her garage, Avis stopped to grab the mail. Once she piled the grocery store coupons and white envelopes under her arm, she let the garage door shut then stepped out of the car.

It was the most ordinary routine in the world, yet it would be the last thing Avis did during her short, bright life.

Gunshots crackled through the suburban garage, literally stopping Avis in her tracks. Bullets struck her in the head, chest, and leg. A fifth shot missed, leaving a black hole where it flew through the garage door and into the street. The ambush was swift and deadly, leaving Avis helpless on the ground, her keys and purse on the floor beside her. Then, swapping the gun for a knife, the intruder stabbed Avis three times before finally slashing her throat, and leaving her cold in a pile of blood, her mail still clutched under her arm.

KEYON PITTMAN FLASHED A QUICK, COY SMILE TOWARD THE BLEACHERS, AND PUT HIS PHONE IN HIS POCKET. He'd spent the majority of basketball practice flirtatiously texting with one of the team members' mothers. The woman's wedding ring caught the light as she sat across the gym, trying not to grin and sneakily texting him back. Amid fumes of adolescent sweat and cheap body spray, the pair carried on like two pre-teens eating up their parents' data plans. Keyon's phone buzzed again at 5:36 p.m., but this time Avis' name flashed across the screen. Keyon answered, briefly discussing dinner plans with his wife-to-be before hanging up and swiftly dialing a third woman, his colleague Carla Hughes.

For Keyon, multitasking was a way of life. He juggled three different jobs—teaching science at Chastain Middle

School, coaching basketball, and occasionally bartending at a restaurant called On the Boarder—and he was similarly capable of juggling several women at a time. With his round, balding head and equally round, beady eyes, he wasn't exactly handsome, but women fell for Keyon's charm, intelligence, and work ethic. Despite his flirtatious nature, he'd managed to build a promising future as a husband and father with Avis. They were on track to become a picture-perfect family, but as the birth of their baby and their planned February wedding drew near, one of Keyon's "casual flirtations" was threatening to complicate things. Lately, Avis noticed that Keyon seemed surgically attached to his phone. On a trip to celebrate Thanksgiving with her family in Houston the week before, Avis' two sisters and parents noticed the trend as well.

"He was on the phone 24/7, all day, all night, in and out the house," Avis' mother Debra Banks said during an interview for an episode of *Dateline*, "Deadly Affair." Avis wasn't happy with Keyon's recent chattiness, and she said as much to him in a text found after her death that read:

I'm doing everything I can to make it work and it will work, but how would you feel if I was on the phone all night?

Still, Keyon was up to his old habits, and after basketball practice that night, he didn't make much of an effort to rush home to his fiancé.

After leaving the school, Keyon drove to the townhouse owned by his fellow teacher, Carla Hughes. The 27-year old taught Language Arts at the middle school and coached cheerleading. Earlier in the day Keyon had been at Carla's to drop off groceries he bought for Avis, and he wanted to pick them up on his way home. Carla's house was located between the school and Avis and Keyon's subdivision, so it made sense—at least to Keyon—that he sometimes dropped groceries there.

Still, the fact that Keyon lingered at another woman's home for about 45 minutes before bringing groceries home to his pregnant fiancé didn't bode well for Keyon's status as a doting future husband. For a man so attached to his phone, Keyon only called Avis twice on Nov. 29, but something must have spooked him—or he was establishing an alibi—because immediately after leaving Carla's house around 8:30 p.m., Keyon called Avis' mother asking if she'd heard from her daughter. Avis' mother, Debra, hadn't heard anything, and by the time Keyon arrived home he must have been very worried, because he told police that when he finally arrived at his house, he opened the garage door automatically from his car, and ran inside the garage—leaving his car's engine running.

He found Avis' body next to the driver's side door of her car. She'd been dead for more than three hours, but remained frozen in the moment she'd left her car. Her car keys and purse lay nearby, and the mail was tucked under her arm. Inside, the house appeared ransacked. Drawers and cabinets were left open and tossed, and a footprint on the door showed where the intruder had kicked it open. Most disturbingly, Avis' pants were pulled down, indicating the possibility of a sex crime in addition to what appeared to be a burglary culminating in murder. It was a gruesome scene, especially for a man who knew this was the woman carrying his baby. Keyon grabbed his phone and frantically dialed for help.

Carla was on the phone with her mother, Linda Banks, when she heard the beep of an incoming call.

"Mom, this is Keyon calling me," Carla said as she checked her screen. When she returned to the call with her mother she hurriedly explained, "They've done—Keyon said that something's happened with Avis. He wants me to go over there."

This was the very first call Keyon made upon finding Avis' body—not to the police, not to Avis' parents or his own parents, but to another woman who wasn't even friends with Avis. As the night continued, his behavior would only turn stranger. After hanging up with Carla, Keyon put away his cell phone and ran to a neighbor's house, acting so frantic that the woman inside thought her own home was being broken into. Startled, the neighbor sent her husband to find out what was going on. Inside, the woman was already on the phone with 9-1-1 when her husband yelled in the background, " somebody killed his wife!" The woman was startled, telling the operator, "Oh my gosh. He says somebody done killed his wife!"

Officers arrived at Keyon and Avis' home quickly, officially transforming the suburban brick house with its Christmas lights and wreath into a crime scene. Some neighbors were gathering outside the garage, and inside Keyon crouched over Avis, making loud sobbing sounds, though no tears seemed to flow down his cheeks. Lt. John Neal of the Ridgeland Police Department was the first officer on the scene, and almost immediately he knew this wasn't a straightforward burglary. Sure, there was a boot print where it looked like someone tried to kick the back door in, clothes and other items were thrown about, and drawers and cabinets were flung open, but on second glance none of it made sense. Big-ticket items like electronics—obvious bait for someone looking to loot the place—were left intact. In the bedroom, dresser drawers were open and despite the intruder's disregard for expensive items, the perpetrator apparently took the time to go through bathroom cabinets full of personal products and household cleaners.

Avis' body provided more clues. Although her pants were pulled down, there was no sign of sexual trauma, and the severity of her wounds—one of the shots made execution style at close range and her throat slashed—indicated that her attacker was fueled by anger and passion. If someone had been caught mid-break-in and was looking to get rid of the witness, they could have silenced Avis without going to such violent efforts.

Attempting to keep him away from the scene and avoid too much chitchat between him and the crowd gathering outside, officers had Keyon wait in a police car as they inspected the scene. He sat distraught, desperate not to leave Avis' body, until authorities finally asked if he could come to the police station to talk over a few things. This was standard practice—after all, Keyon was the closest person to the victim as well as the first witness to find her body—but Keyon was none-to-happy to be answering questions upstairs while his friends and family waited downstairs.

"Hold on, let me call you right back," Keyon said, pressing his cellphone to his ear and crouching in his seat as Detective Frank Dillard entered the room where suspects and witnesses were grilled.

"You can continue talking if you want to," Det. Dillard told him, but Keyon hung up anyway. The interview between Keyon and Det. Dillard stretched late into the night. It revealed a stunning contradiction in Keyon, a man comfortable enough to text and chat with someone he referred to as "Babe" inside the police interview room, but defensive enough to rant about being "guilty 'til proven innocent." By the time the interview ended, Keyon refused to sign a Miranda warning and he found a lawyer within 24 hours.

In a vacuum, some of Keyon's behavior could be written off as the actions of a man who was distraught and off-balance after enduring a grisly tragedy. Taken together though, Keyon's choices leading up to and after his fiancé's murder practically screamed of guilt. Maybe running to a neighbor's house instead of using his own cellphone to call police wasn't odd for someone in shock, but using the cellphone to call another woman *first* definitely was. Being suspicious of a police interview wasn't so crazy, but calling someone "Babe" over the phone a few hours after losing your fiancé and unborn child —there's no explaining that behavior away.

Investigators had every reason to think Keyon was guilty of something, but there was one major problem. All of those flirtatious text messages and phone calls that made Keyon such a lousy fiancé also gave him a perfect alibi. Phone records showed that Keyon had in fact been at basketball practice the night of Avis' murder, and while some eyewitnesses said he left early, police couldn't charge Keyon with a murder without placing him at the scene. Who else then, if not the lying, cheating fiancé, would have wanted this woman dead?

CARLA STARED ACROSS THE TABLE AT DET. DILLARD, OCCASIONALLY WRITING NOTES and pushing her long, dark hair behind her ear. She looked put together and pretty, especially when her business-like demeanor momentarily cracked, revealing a warm smile and a small, breezy laugh. It was two days since Avis' murder and the detective had approached her at school after investigators noticed her name popping up as a close acquaintance and possible girlfriend of Keyon's. At the time, Carla seemed too overcome with emotion to offer a proper interview. She had left the police department, then voluntarily returned that evening, and was now walking Det. Dillard through a detailed timeline of Keyon's every move on the day of his fiancé's death. She appeared focused, cradling her chin in her hand thoughtfully and occasionally making notes like an honor student working through an oral exam.

Carla Hughes: I first spoke with him that morning before work, and talked to him off and on during work.

Det. Dillard: Thought cellphones weren't allowed at the, at the school?

CH: No, we work in the same building.

DD: Oh, that's right. (Carla laughs.)

CH: So yeah, we um, on and off at work and then we talked right after work, after we dismissed the kids. And then he told me he was fixin' to go to the grocery store and then he'd uh, be at my house right after that. So I went home, he went to, you know, he said he was going to the grocery store, and at four o clock—around four or five—he was at my house. He came to my house with the groceries. And he sat at my house for about an hour or so. He left at 5:10—said he was going to basketball practice. And he said, 'OK, well I'll be back after practice to pick up the groceries, you know, before I go home.' So I said OK. I started grading papers He came by around 7:35 or something like that. He stayed about 45 minutes. He went home. For enough time for him to leave home and leave my house and get home he called me. I thought he was calling to say he made it home, you know, whatever, and he called me screaming.

DD: Is that unusual for, for him to does he normally call you when he gets home, say 'Hey I made it home'?

Despite Carla's repeated claims that she and Keyon were just good friends, Det. Dillard now knew there was far more going on. Co-workers from On the Border, where Keyon occasionally bartended, had seen Carla and Keyon being openly affectionate. At school, teachers and students said Carla and Keyon acted like a couple, and some reported that they'd used students to pass messages back and forth throughout the day.

An affair didn't necessarily make anyone a murderer, but lying about it repeatedly during a police investigation didn't look good, and it was clear from Carla's interview that she and Keyon were more than close—they were practically inseparable. Try as she might to keep up the "just friends" routine, Det. Dillard was on to Carla, and eventually, when he asked yet again if she and Keyon were involved, she said yes. Now, it was time for Det. Dillard to put the pressure on.

DD: Well why did you lie to me earlier?

CH: I didn't lie to you.

DD: Yes, I simply asked if y'all were romantically involved. You said 'No'.

CH: I said we were close friends.

DD: And I asked if y'all were romantically involved. You said 'No'.

CH: I don't remember saying no. I just said we were close friends. But I don't wanna argue with you, it's not that I'm trying to hide anything.

The two went back and forth a while longer, but Det. Dillard had heard all he needed to for now. Thanks to Carla's admission, investigators now had concrete proof that Keyon was unfaithful, that Keyon and Carla were capable of lying, and that they'd been in contact both before and after the time of Avis' murder.

What Det. Dillard didn't know yet, was what else Carla had lied to him about. When he'd asked her if she owned or had access to any guns, Carla told him no, but as soon as the interview was finished, she was on her way to return a revolver she'd borrowed only four days earlier.

Carla's cousin, Patrick Nash, examined the Rossi .38 caliber gun he'd lent her. While returning it, Carla mentioned that police had visited her at school that day. Patrick was uneasy. His mind flashed to the chat he and Carla had on Nov. 26, when she dropped by his house and told him how concerned she was about recent break-in attempts at her townhouse. Patrick suggested Carla get some mace to strap on her purse, but she was thinking of something a bit more serious.

"How many guns do you have?" she'd asked. Knowing Carla was a young woman living alone in a tough neighborhood, Patrick agreed to lend her his gun, along with five bullets and a hunting knife. It was a gesture meant to make Carla feel more comfortable. But just three days later she called to pass along the news that Keyon's fiancé had been shot and murdered. That was enough to give Patrick an uneasy feeling. His father, James Nash, became aware of the situation, and wasted no time beating around the bush with his niece. Carla's uncle asked her flat-out if the gun had anything to do with Avis' murder, and her reaction—saying nothing, bowing her head and shrugging—was far from comforting.

Now, as Patrick looked over the returned gun (he told Carla she could keep the knife) he knew something was very wrong. The five bullets he'd given her were all missing. Carla claimed that she'd gone target practicing, but she'd misjudged her cousin and uncle. No one in her family had any intention of getting caught on the wrong side of a murder investigation, and on Dec. 5th Patrick turned the gun over to police, breaking the case wide open.

Once investigators had the gun, they wasted little time.

Shell casings recovered from the crime scene were consistent with a Rossi .38 caliber revolver, and Patrick's story about the five missing bullets accounted for the four shots to Avis' body plus one through the garage door. When ballistics tests came back positive, it was clear that this was, in fact, the murder weapon. Police pulled Carla back in for questioning on Dec. 6th—the day after receiving the gun—with enough evidence to charge her with being an accessory after the fact.

Their real goal was still to get something on Keyon. Results from the lab showed traces of gunpowder residue on each of his palms, and they had photos of his clothes that day stained with Avis' blood. That, combined with a mountain of circumstantial evidence, made Keyon a tantalizing target, but without more information their hands were tied. He could have picked up the gunpowder residue and blood when he touched Avis' body after finding her, plus he still had a pretty solid alibi for that night. Still, investigators now had Carla on the hook, and with a little pressure she seemed likely to turn on the man who had probably gotten her into this mess.

Carla arrived at the police department for more questioning looking the worse for wear. Gone was the self-assured confidence and flirtatious demeanor, replaced by a passive woman, staring down toward the table in a messy ponytail and sweatshirt. She was armed with a lawyer named Johnnie Walls, a man with a large, imposing presence, who seemed to care deeply about Carla. By day, Carla's lawyer was actually a state senator from her hometown, Greenville, Miss. He was a friend of the Hughes family hoping to help a young woman who seemed to have somehow gotten very off track from the promising life she'd always led.

After stepping outside to speak with investigators, Walls returned to have a private chat with Carla. Inside the interview room, a small camera discretely recorded him explaining to his client that she might be able to get a good deal if she'd just provide some information about Keyon. Try as he might to convince her, Carla refused to make any statements implicating herself or Keyon in the crime.

Johnnie Walls: You can stop them from charging you if you put the finger on him, and he (referring, presumably, one of the detectives) can't understand why you won't do that. He says, 'She must be in love with this cat.' And I said, 'Well, I don't know. Maybe she is.'

Carla Hughes: It's not that. I mean, if I don't—if I wasn't there when he did it, then I just wasn't there when he did. I can't make myself say he did it if I don't know. I just know he wasn't with me.

Police searched her townhome for more evidence linking her or Keyon to Avis' murder. They recovered a love poem with the initials K.P., a framed picture of Keyon in Carla's bedroom, and a pair of women's work boots matching the tread pattern left on the backdoor of Avis' house. Meanwhile, the same phone records that placed Keyon at the school on the evening of Feb. 29th also placed Carla near Avis' home a few minutes before and after the murder.

The call Keyon made to Carla—right after Avis' call to let Keyon know she was almost home—bounced off a tower near Keyon and Avis' house. A second call from Carla to Keyon about half an hour later bounced off the same tower, and after that Carla was on her way back to her own house to meet Keyon after practice.

Carla, originally charged with accessory to murder, now faced capital murder charges.

All of the evidence seemed then, as it still does today, to point to some kind of collusion between Keyon and Carla in Avis' murder. Even if one of them did it on their own, the other would have surely figured it out long before speaking with police. Perhaps this was a case of true love: two people sticking together, unwilling to ever implicate one another in the gruesome deed they'd done. But Keyon wasn't man enough to speak up and share the responsibility, either.

STANDING BEFORE THE COURTROOM WITH HIS HAND HELD HIGH, KEYON PITTMAN looked especially small. His blank expression evaporated as he took the witness stand, moaning and sniffing as he dabbed at his eyes with a tissue. Squint and whimper as he might, Keyon's cheeks remained tellingly dry. Carla stared unblinkingly forward. Three years older now, she looked elegant in a dark tweed jacket and polished up-do, but where a friendly glow once warmed her face, Carla's expression now appeared dull, disillusioned, and worn out. She was on trial for two counts of murder: one for Avis, and another for Avis' unborn baby. An autopsy had concluded Avis was expecting a boy. If convicted, Carla could face the death penalty.

Keyon was the defense's chief witness against his former coworker and lover. He admitted he had started to see Carla just one month after learning Avis was pregnant.

"There was no long term. There was, there was sexual, caught up in the moment—speaking for myself—there, there never was a long-term plan with Carla," Keyon testified. He went on to paint a picture of a woman obsessed. He told the jury about the time Carla claimed to be pregnant and threatened to go to Avis, and described Carla basically stalking him despite his refusal to break off his engagement. Just before Avis died, during a visit with

Keyon's mother in Picayune, Miss., the weekend after Thanksgiving, Keyon said that Carla drove out and rented a hotel room, hoping she and Keyon could spend time together. Keyon actually left Avis with his mother to meet Carla, but according to him, when he told her he'd have to get back to his fiancé she became upset. "It ended on a bad note," he told the jury.

Carla, on the other hand, did not testify. While her defense team pointed out Keyon's poor character and the important fact that he had a key to Carla's house, giving him possible access to the boots and weapons used in Avis' murder, Carla maintained her long silence. As the jury delivered its verdict days later, the courtroom let out a collective gasp. Convicted on two counts of capital murder, Carla would now have to fight for her right to live.

Under different circumstances, the two women involved in this ugly ordeal might have gone on to change a lot of kids' lives. Avis studied early childhood education and dreamed of starting her own daycare, helping raise entire classrooms of children while she brought up her little boy at home. She and Carla were both Mississippi born and raised, both smart as a whip, and both committed to education.

Carla, during the years before her affair with Keyon, was an incredibly ambitious young woman. She'd competed in several college sports, made the dean's list and the mayor's youth council, competed in major beauty pageants, and placed sixth in the world while showing and riding Tennessee walking horses. She was on her way to completing a PhD when she fell down the dark rabbit hole of love and violence that led her to that Mississippi courtroom.

Avis, like Carla, was a high achiever. She was the first of three siblings to graduate from college, a beloved middle sister who couldn't wait to have her family over for the first Christmas she and Keyon would celebrate in their new home.

Sadly, in addition to their beauty and intelligence, Avis and Carla shared a dark undercurrent of love-gone-wrong. Just as Avis was pregnant and engaged, Carla had once been too. Around the time she graduated college, Carla became pregnant, and was planning to marry the father. Unfortunately, the wedding never happened and Carla was left to raise her child alone while starting her career as a teacher. None of this slowed Carla down. She persevered, as she'd always done before, continuing her studies and finding a good job at Chastain Middle School, but it left a wound that may have become infected as she watched the man she loved come closer and closer to giving Avis the life and wedding Carla never had.

In the end, while Avis' life was lost, Carla's was spared. On October 13, 2009, Carla was handed two life sentences in a Mississippi prison. Upon hearing the verdict, Carla and Avis' fathers actually shared a tearful, brief hug—two men forever tied by a deep sense of loss.

While she has filed appeals, Carla is yet to break her silence about Keyon's involvement. In fact, one year before her trial, Mississippi investigators sent Carla a little Valentine's gift: one last plea to help them convict the man they've always suspected was behind his fiancé's murder. The envelope contained a photocopy of a marriage certificate belonging to Keyon and his new bride.

Less than a year after Avis' death and Carla's being charged with murder, Keyon was married. According to Johnnie Walls, his client's only response to the tragic valentine was to say simply, 'I'm not surprised.'

The Last Breath

Jeffrey Havard and Shaken Baby Syndrome

JEFFREY HAVARD SAT DAZED ON THE FLOOR OF HIS TRAILER watching his girlfriend, Rebecca Britt, kneel over her helpless baby daughter.

Rebecca performed infant CPR, pushing on the child's sternum and counting *one and two and three and four and...* The baby's chest rose and fell while her mother blew air into her mouth but it was hopeless; six-month-old Chloe Britt was blue and limp and dying. Despite Rebecca's best efforts, her little girl was as good as gone.

If not for Chloe's death, February 21st, 2002 would have been a pretty unremarkable day in Jeff and Becky's lives. Both 23 years old and unemployed, neither of them had anywhere very important to be. But motivated to change, Becky was out the door by 10 a.m. to drop Chloe off at Grace United Methodist Church for daycare before heading to a grocery store to pick up a job application. The daycare workers—who saw Chloe on a regular basis—noticed nothing out of the ordinary aside from some flu-like symptoms stemming from a recent ear infection.

Around mid-day, Becky made the 45-minute drive north from Natchez, Miss. to Alcorn State University in Lorman, where she was considering going back to school. When she returned to the trailer around 2:30 p.m. to look over the purple and gold ASU information packets, Jeff was still sleeping. Peacefully dreaming the day away, Jeff had no idea of the nightmare to come.

When Becky returned to the church around 5:30 p.m. to pick up Chloe, the child was still fine, aside from her general fussiness. An employee who changed the baby's diaper before sending her off noticed some diaper rash, but found nothing else noteworthy about the child's physical condition. Jeff finally woke up once Becky and the baby came home, and got to work collecting dirty dishes and onesies while Becky gave Chloe medicine and tried to cheer her up.

Chloe wasn't Jeff's biological daughter. She and Becky had moved into the trailer about three weeks before, only two months after Becky and Jeff met. Regardless, Jeff seemed to be a helpful and caring presence in Becky and Chloe's lives. He cleaned up messes, changed diapers, and made bottles without putting up a fuss. Asked later if Jeff ever acted angry toward her child, Becky would tell police, "No, he loved her." So, when Jeff handed Becky some money and asked her to go grab dinner for them, she didn't think twice about leaving Chloe in his care. She fed Chloe some bananas, placed her in an infant swing, and headed out for 45 minutes without any concern.

According to Jeff, that's when disaster struck. Just a few minutes after her mother left, the peaceful baby began to squirm and cry. Jeff started to change her diaper, but realized she was totally dry. Still crying—a mix of tears and nasal mucus running down her face—Chloe spit up on herself. Not sure what was wrong, Jeff decided to give her a bath and rub her down with lavender lotion, a routine he'd watched Becky perform before putting the infant to bed. He placed Chloe in her infant tub just as he'd watched Becky do, hoping to have her asleep by the time her mother got back from the store.

As he stood over the tub and began lifting Chloe out, the wet baby slipped from Jeff's grasp. Her head slammed into the porcelain toilet bowl, her leg hit the lid, and her upper body collided with the tank. Too late, Jeff caught the child and swung her up, terrified to see what he'd done. "As soon as she hit, she just gasped for air like it sacred her or like it put her into a shock or something," he later told Adams County Deputy John Manley. Still panicking, he gently twisted the baby and held her head as he gave her a little shake, hoping to rouse her out of shock. Once the child seemed to be breathing and alert, Jeff placed her on the bed to try and get back to his planned routine.

His hands still shaking, it took Jeff two tries to put Chloe in a diaper without tearing the adjustable tabs. He rubbed the clean baby with lavender lotion, only to have her spit up most of her dinner—along with a reddish-pink substance Jeff assumed to be medicine—all over the bed sheets. Jeff wiped the baby off, put her in a nightshirt, and placed her in her crib, still troubled by the earlier incident. Becky returned to find him letting out bathwater and removing the sheets. Jeff clenched up as his girlfriend tiptoed into the baby's room to see how she was doing.

"She made a funny noise in her throat like she was coughing up a hairball or something like that," Becky said, describing seeing her baby. "And I picked her up and patted her on the back and made sure there wasn't anything in her throat. She was fine, she was breathing fine, her color was fine. I put her back in bed."

When Becky returned from Chloe's room unalarmed, Jeff felt assured the baby must have been all right. He decided not to mention the fall, knowing it would only make Becky upset. Instead, he handed her another twenty-dollar bill and asked her to make a run to Blockbuster for some movies. By the time Becky came home around 9:30 p.m. Jeff was in the bathroom with the door shut. Becky checked to make sure Chloe was sleeping and quickly realized something was wrong. Chloe's throat was swollen shut and she wasn't getting any air. Yelling for Jeff, Becky placed the child on the ground and administered infant CPR. Her mother, a nurse at Natchez Community Hospital, had taught her the procedure just in case. After five rounds, Becky, Jeff, and the baby jumped into the car and flew to the hospital—a startled Jeff still neglecting to mention Chloe's earlier accident.

Screaming, "My baby's not breathing!" Becky passed the baby to nurses and doctors who crowded around the infant's swollen, blue body. Physicians noticed her eyes fixed and dilated and suspected bleeding in her brain. When they began to insert a rectal thermometer, they noticed that Chloe's anus was dilated to about the size of a quarter—it was gaping open.

In addition, Chloe had bruising and abrasions that hinted at some kind of abuse. When asked by a nurse about the last people in contact with Chloe, Becky replied that the child was in her care—and Jeff's—all day. At the hospital staff's request, a security officer accompanied Jeff to the waiting room.

Meanwhile, Jeff *still* hadn't mentioned Chloe's fall. Even after doctors pronounced the baby dead, he kept the critical incident to himself, perhaps hampering doctors' ability to treat the child, and certainly derailing the imminent investigation. Two days later, after forty-eight hours of despair over the dead baby girl, Jeff approached investigators. While he planned to confess to a tragic accident, Jeff would be questioned in relation to something much worse: the molestation and murder of a six-month-old child.

"OK, HOW HARD DID YOU SHAKE HER?"

Jeff may not have known it, but Deputy Manley's question was a one-way ticket down a very dangerous path. In his statement to Manley, Jeff explained the bathroom accident.

"I dropped her, and she just kind of gasped for air like I had scared her, or I don't know what happened. So I took her and I shook her. I didn't shake her hard. I don't think I did. I shook her back and forth from the side like this, sideways, and twisted her like that. Shook her—you know—twisted her like that, shaking her. She started crying again, so I said, 'Okay, she's alright.' I put her on my shoulder and patted her butt, telling her I was sorry. I am sorry."

Jeff's use of the term "shake" would be his undoing.

"I shook her I didn't shake her hard I shook her back and forth."

He was trying to say that he had attempted to rouse her. But "shake" meant something else to law enforcement.

For years, shaken-baby syndrome, sometimes known as shaken infant syndrome, has served as a magic bullet for explaining mysterious infant deaths and placing caregivers behind bars. While social workers and pediatricians often remain adamant about the true cases in which such trauma has resulted in life-altering or life-ending outcomes, more and more science reveals the problematic aspects of such a diagnosis.

At the core of any SBS case is a classic "triad" of symptoms: bleeding between the brain and skull, bleeding behind the retinas, and swelling of the brain. As the theory goes, this triad of symptoms is exclusively caused by violently shaking a child. For almost forty years, medical examiners who noticed the three crucial symptoms without obvious signs of external trauma, immediately jumped to SBS in their quest to determine a cause of death.

Beyond its implications in labs and courtrooms, the introduction of SBS became prompted a cultural phenomenon. Parents, terrified that one day their babysitter might snap at the sound of one more cry for a diaper change, began installing "nanny cams" in innocent-looking nursery teddy bears. Television shows portrayed suit-clad attorneys passionately shaking baby dolls before a shocked jury, demonstrating the cruel fury that engulfed some unfit parent or caregiver.

Studies completed during the past few years pose questions for the infallibility of SBS, despite the fact that people all over the country are already behind bars based on the diagnosis. For starters, some experts claim that it is physically impossible for a human to shake a child with enough force to cause the listed symptoms. More complicated, is the argument that after being shaken, a baby could remain lucid for hours and possibly days—making it impossible for doctors to pinpoint the time of an incident and implicate a particular caregiver.

Other critics say that while the diagnosis may be pertinent in certain cases, other factors could cause similar symptoms, so physicians and medical examiners should keep an open mind when presented with the classic triad of symptoms. Trauma from a fall as low as two or three feet, like the one Jeff described in Chloe's case, is a named alternative. Even when no external injuries are present, some experts say, infection and re-bleeds associated with birth defects and complications can have similar outcomes as those found in shaken infants.

In Mississippi, at least 11 people have been tried and prosecuted for infant deaths related to SBS, with two people waiting on death row. While SBS is a problematic and widely used diagnosis around the country, one man, in particular, made Mississippi an especially dubious battleground for those fighting life or death sentences.

FOR ABOUT TWENTY YEARS, THE VAST MAJORITY OF DEAD BODIES in Mississippi passed before a single set of eyes, those of the now infamous Dr. Steven T. Hayne.

Looking back, Jeffrey Havard—guilty or not—was doomed the second Hayne laid Chloe Britt atop his autopsy table in 2002. Here was a man with an astonishing reach of power despite monstrously oversized caseloads and an absence of basic credentials. Jeff, with hardly any resources to fight back, was about to be legally bulldozed.

Never certified by the American Board of Pathology, Hayne's work as a privately contracted pathologist was prolific and in many ways problematic. While the National Association of Medical Examiners (NAME) recommends that doctors avoid critical mistakes by limiting themselves to about 250 autopsies per year (with 325 representing the absolute limit) Hayne performed upward of 1,200 autopsies annually—peaking at nearly 1,800 in a single year. His booming private business between the late 1980's and about 2008 may have had something to do with his knack for helping Mississippi prosecutors earn convictions based on his testimony.

Hayne's reign as Mississippi's primary pathologist for so many years was not lacking in the type of critical errors NAME warned against with their guidelines. From making notes about removing the ovaries and uterus of a victim who happened to be male, to reportedly weighing kidneys that were removed from the patient years earlier, the doctor's work included a handful of baffling slip-ups. Most troubling, is the fact that Hayne's oversized workload and the mistakes that resulted were no secret to Mississippi officials. Rather than question his practices, officials allowed Hayne to continue serving as a crucial witness in the state's cases, helping secure jail-time and in some cases death sentences for those accused of severe crimes.

When Jeff went to trial in December, 2002, Hayne's poor reputation prompted Jeff's public defender, Robert Clark, to request funding for an independent review of the autopsy report. Just as it has in at least two other cases similar to Jeff's, the Mississippi legal system denied Jeff's request, leaving Hayne undisputed as the state's final and most damning witness.

Hayne testified that Jeff had sexually abused Chloe, likely by forcing an object up the infant's rectum. As for the ultimate cause of death, he said there was "lethal" bleeding inside Chloe's skull, including subdural hemorrhaging (blood between Chloe's brain and skull), and bleeding behind her eyes. This child, Hayne claimed, was shaken violently until she bled internally to death.

Oddly, the controversial doctor, who testified in several other SBS cases, failed to even identify the traditional triad of SBS symptoms in his examination of Chloe's body. Explaining to the jury the classic signs of an SBS related death, Hayne testified, " the classic triad for shaken baby syndrome is one, the presence of a subdural hemorrhage; and, two, the presence of retinal hemorrhage; and, three, the absence of other potentially lethal causes of death." In fact, the three classic signs of SBS named by most experts include brain swelling, which Hayne failed to identify or mention in relation to Chloe's examination. Of course, because Jeff was denied the access to an independent medical examiner's testimony, the jury had only Hayne's word—backed by statements from doctors and nurses at the hospital—to base their decision on.

Other factors weakened Jeff's case even more, almost guaranteeing him a cell on Mississippi's death row.

During opening statements, Assistant District Attorney Tom Rosenblatt effectively introduced Chloe as "a precious six-month-old baby girl" before swiftly working through the timeline of events that lead to her tragic death. In turn, Jeff's public defender stumbled through his presentation, introducing extraneous ideas and correcting himself each time he misspoke.

"You were also told that Ms. Britt doesn't work. That Jeffery had worked, but he had given up his job on the river as a deckhand. If you know anything about working on a river like that, that's quite—you're out for a long period of time, usually forty-five to sixty days. It's not conducive for a relationship so—with another person. Now about 7:45 that evening, Mr. Britt—I mean Mrs. Britt, went to Natchez Market to get groceries as Mr. Rosenblatt told you," the public defender rambled on. He never offered much of a stirring rebuttal for a client facing execution.

On top of this, few people remained by Jeff's side in the wake of such ugly allegations. Becky, after being told by investigators that Jeff had molested and shaken her sweet child, served as a witness for the prosecution. While the state offered sixteen witnesses during the guilt phase of the trial, the defense managed to offer up only one. Lasting only four days from start to finish, Jeff's trial provided almost no resistance to the state's crushing allegations. After less than an hour of deliberation, the jury found Jeffrey Havard guilty on all charges. After receiving the death sentence, he headed to Parchment Penitentiary to slowly await the end of his life at the state's hands.

A DECADE AFTER CHLOE BRITT WAS FOUND DEAD in her bed, the *Jackson Clarion-Ledger* dusted off the case. At the paper's request, Dr. Michael Baden, the former Chief Medical Examiner of New York City and Chief Forensic Pathologist for the New York State Police, reviewed the evidence that years earlier helped a jury convict Jeff. After assessing Chloe's birth, pediatric, and medical records, as well as testimony by the emergency room doctors and Hayne's autopsy report, Baden responded,

"In my opinion, Chloe Britt's death is entirely consistent with a short fall, and not with an abusive shaking Chloe's signs and symptoms did not establish the classic triad of Shaken Baby Syndrome—a condition which now many forensic pathologists have concluded does not exist; and who now conclude that scientific evidence shows that shaking a baby cannot produce subdural hemorrhages or sufficient brain damage to cause a baby to die Furthermore, the autopsy findings and testimony concluding there were intentional anal injuries was premature and short-sighted. The anus can dilate in a coma or after death, and any anal abrasion could be due to innocent causes, such as constipation or diarrhea. If the child was deceased prior to arriving at the hospital, the anal dilation seen by doctors at the hospital and in the autopsy could have been natural changes in the body upon death From my analysis, Chloe was not sexually assaulted and she died of injuries consistent with an accidental drop. I base this conclusion on the medical record and recent medical literature, and I hold this opinion to a reasonable degree of medical certainty."

Baden wasn't the first credible pathologist to refute

Hayne's findings. Years earlier, Alabama State Medical Examiner Jim Lauridson reexamined Hayne's autopsy and found it similarly lacking in evidence of SBS or sexual assault. Ironically, in 2006 the Mississippi Supreme Court refused to allow Jeff to introduce Lauridson's findings as new evidence, ruling that the report should have been produced during the initial trial—the same trial in which the court refused Jeff funding for an opinion from an independent medical examiner.

Most surprisingly of all, was Hayne's own critique of his original findings, when in 2009, he acknowledged there was no sufficient evidence that sexual assault had taken place. Later, he back peddled from the SBS diagnosis as well, citing recent studies that show humans lack the force required to provoke the deadly triad of SBS symptoms. In 2008, much to his dismay, the state of Mississippi finally pulled the rug out from Hayne's practice. Rather than charging him with wrongdoing, they quietly asked him to step down, leaving thousands of criminals eager to appeal their Hayne-based convictions.

Jeffrey Havard, now 36 years old, has been the subject of many news articles. A group called Free Jeffrey Havard maintains a website detailing the problems with Jeff's trial, and the Mississippi Innocence Project shed light on his case in their fierce critique of Hayne's practices.

Jeffrey Havard is guilty of covering up a horrible accident. He could be guilty—or innocent—of more. Certainly, he is the victim of a messy, ineffective, and unfair legal system. Mississippi has just begun to improve its criminal justice system in the years since his 2002 trial.

The way has been cleared for new appeals. For now, Jeffrey Havard remains on Mississippi's death row.

Photo Archive

Stephanie Tate-Kennedy thought she had hit the jackpot when she met surgeon Dr. David Stephens. Only her marriage and his wife stood between her and a mansion.

When David Stephens died, he was buried beside his first wife, Karen.
There was no room for Stephanie.

Ouida Keeton was an audacious Southern belle. You could say she loved her mother to pieces.

The 'Legs' trial received sensational news coverage.

Reunited at last, Ouida is buried next to her mother, or what was left of her mother.

Who would want to kill cheerful, pregnant, child care worker Avis Banks?

Middle school teacher Carla Ann Hughes took too much interest in Avis' fiancé.

Police thought Keyon Pittman was involved in his fiancés murder. But he was never charged, and ultimately testified against Carla Hughes.

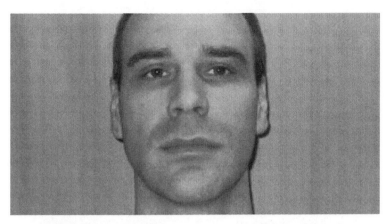

Jeffrey Havard was convicted of murdering his girlfriend's six-month old daughter. He is on death row.

Controversial medical examiner Steven Hayne concluded that the baby girl died of Shaken Baby Syndrome. He's come under fire for what the Washington Post called "his sloppy practices."

The Mississippi Supreme Court ruled that Havard can challenge his murder conviction. Other cases, in Mississippi and across the country, are also being re-examined based on recent scientific developments.

About the Authors

RON FRANSCELL is the bestselling crime author of The Darkest Night and Delivered from Evil. His work has also appeared in the Washington Post, San Francisco Chronicle, Chicago Sun-Times, Denver Post, and others. He has been praised by Ann Rule, Vincent Bugliosi and other true-crime heavyweights as one of the most provocative new voices in narrative nonfiction.

STEPHANIE COOK is a free-lance writer in Seattle. She was a reporter for the *Durango Herald* and news editor of the *Fort Lewis College Independent*, both in Durango, Colorado.

GREGG OLSEN is the *New York Times* bestselling author of twenty books, both true crime and fiction, including *Shocking True Story, Fear Collector, A Twisted Faith, Starvation Heights,* and *If Loving You Is Wrong.*

REBECCA MORRIS is the author of *Ted and Ann – The Mystery of a Missing Child and Her Neighbor Ted Bundy,* and *Bad Apples – Inside the Teacher/Student Sex Scandal Epidemic.*

Gregg and Rebecca are the authors of *If I Can't Have You – Susan Powell, Her Mysterious Disappearance and the Murder of Her Children,* and the New York Times bestselling *Bodies of Evidence,* the first book in the Notorious USA series.

Their new book, *A Killing in Amish Country*, will be published by St. Martin's in 2016.

If there's a notorious case you'd like us to write about—anywhere in the country—contact us.

Gregg@GreggOlsen.com

And find out more about the Notorious USA series at our website:

www.notorioususa.com

INTRIGUE DRAMA SUSPENSE

Don't miss these Crime Rant classics.
www.crimerant.com

Made in the USA
Middletown, DE
01 December 2017